Babs Behan

Photography by Kim Lightbody

BOT ANI CAL INKS

**Plant-to-Print
Dyes, Techniques
and Projects**

quadrille

CONTENTS

THE AUTHOR

I first became aware of natural dyeing and printing processes when a friend told me about a vegetable dye block-printing factory in India. I had studied BA Surface Design at the University of the Arts London, but was concerned about all the synthetic chemicals that were used, which got on my skin and offset into the air. When I arrived at the studio each day I was hit by a wall of toxic vapour and it didn't feel safe to be working in this way for long periods of time. I wanted to find a more sustainable and natural way forward, so I arranged an internship in Jaipur, India, at the factory my friend had visited. It turned out to be a fascinating and life-changing experience.

Murghal-style block printing has an elegant look: hand-carved teak blocks and vegetable inks create delicate prints on cloth and Khadi paper. It's a practice that has been handed down through generations, but is now mostly a vanishing tradition due to the increasing demand for synthetic screen- and roll-printing. I fell in love with the quality of line the wooden blocks produced, the earthy colours of the syrupy plant dyes, the skill of the artisans and the sophistication of their hand-crafted work.

I learned how to carve wooden blocks based on my own illustrations, to play with repeat patterns and to use vegetable inks on cotton and silk. I also discovered the vintage silk sari recycling industry, which seemed a more sustainable way to produce clothing – using cloth that already existed and had a second life left in it, rather than creating more. This led me to create a clothing line that focused on using natural fibres and recycling vintage cloth into colourful, expressive, bohemian garments, which I sold through independent boutiques in the UK.

Meanwhile, I travelled to explore other cultures and different ways of living and seeing the world – and I was fascinated to find that dyeing using plant materials is still thriving in many areas. Everywhere I went, I learned what I could about the natural dyes specific to each place. In Laos, I made dyes using madder and indigo, and dyed skeins of peace silk with traditional textile institution Ock Pop Tok to make the most

lustrous shades of blood red and midnight blue. In the Sacred Valley of Peru, I stayed for a week with a Quetchuan master dyer in his family home at 2,000 metres altitude, where we brewed large cauldrons of plant material into vibrant shades of bright pink, soft turquoise, deep green, scarlet red and mustard yellow. In Indonesia, I explored batik painting with wax on bolts of cotton. In southern India, I learned about their natural dyeing and weaving industry.

After six years of the travelling artisan lifestyle, I was ready for a change. International supply chains no longer made any sense to me – instead I dreamed of the re-emergence of a local manufacturing system, using locally sourced fibre and natural plant dyes. I spent the summer of 2013 on an artist residency in the Cotswolds, developing a palette of dyes made from local hedgerow plants. I loved the magic of creating colour from the plants around me, infused with their unique herbal essences. I created clothing that spoke of the land; my wardrobe became filled with meaningful garments, which gave me a sense of place and felt restorative and empowering, like herbal charms. I began to teach what I had learned to others, sharing with them the pleasure of foraging plants for colour and connecting with nature in a new and interesting way.

This led me to found Botanical Inks, an artisan natural dye studio based in Bristol, England. The studio specialises in creating organic, naturally dyed and printed cloth and paper for local designers, and offers workshops in contemporary and traditional dyeing and printing techniques. My intention is to raise awareness of the ecological and social issues involved in making things, and to provide viable non-toxic, low-impact solutions.

Botanical Inks allows me to demonstrate what is possible with natural materials and techniques. And ultimately, I hope that this work can encourage cultural change in the way we create things. That we will re-adopt some of the old tried and tested processes, and combine them with our contemporary skills and technology, so that we can work in a way that is more responsible for people and planet.

BOTANICAL INKS

There is so much joy that comes from colour and nature. My studio, Botanical Inks, was founded in order to explore what's available in the natural world, and to reduce the impact of the textile and creative industries on the environment and people.

Botanical Inks first began by offering workshops in the natural dye techniques I had learned and developed from my travels, with an emphasis on using materials and tools that are of the earth, are safe to work with and that can safely be put back into the earth at the end of their useful lifecycle. I like to work with local farmers, growers, weavers and mills to source and use 100% organic, natural dyes, mordants, cloth and paper. I also use natural fibre tools, such as wooden printing blocks, brushes and string. The people who attend the workshops seem to respond to these holistic, authentic practices and this way of extracting colours from plants. They feel inspired by making natural dyes, paints, drawing and printing inks, and using them in textile and paper surface design techniques.

Understanding the natural colour palette of a particular bio-region, and creating art with materials that you have made with your own hands and from the plants that grow around you, can be an incredibly enriching, empowering and connective experience. There is something simple and beautiful about walking out onto the land and picking up fallen leaves, harvesting flowers and berries, and digging up muddy roots, and then soaking them in water to extract their colour.

I have seen people falling in love over and over again with these old-new ways of creating something – they love the fact that bringing more beauty into the world needn't be harmful to the environment or to their own personal health.

I have a drive to share these skills, because they are otherwise not easily found. I want to make it easier for others to use natural materials for their creative pursuits, and for those in industry to see that it is commercially viable for their work, too.

Following the popularity of the workshops, Botanical Inks started creating limited-edition handmade naturally dyed products and bespoke services. These include bundle-dyed silk scarves; a bridal bouquet recycling service to make silk lingerie and keepsakes; waste food-dyed table linens; wild writing inks; and block-printed gift cards. These not only add something radical to the marketplace and challenge the status quo, but also demonstrate the high level of sustainable practice that is really possible in the UK.

It feels important to create a local system like this, not only for the environment, but also society. It's amazing to be able to invest in something made within the community, using local resources and the traditional skills that are characteristic of the culture. It strengthens a sense of community, as well as the relationship with the local land and nature.

For people at home, starting out on a small scale, perhaps this last point about connecting with nature is truly key. Modern life involves more time spent indoors, with less opportunity to interact with plants, animals and wild landscapes. Spending time outdoors – and developing playful relationships with natural materials – may be a way to reconnect with our environment and to cultivate an affinity for the natural world. Botanical Inks has allowed me to do this, and I hope this book helps you to do the same.

HOW TO USE THIS BOOK

This book has been written as a guide and companion for the home dyer – natural dyeing isn't an exact science, and there is no one right way to do it. It's best to travel through the book from front to back, as the first two chapters, Fibres, Mordants and Modifiers, and Making Dyes, provide you with all the basic information you need to get started. Much of the book refers back to these chapters, which cover how to prepare your fabrics, as well as how to make and use dye baths. The Dye Colours chapter goes on to list some of the most popular dye materials you can find or buy, and gives an overview of their characteristics, as well as tips on how to prepare and use them. The Dyeing Techniques chapter explores applying natural colour and print to textiles. And lastly, the Projects chapter offers a selection of ideas to help you turn your dyed textiles into wonderful gifts and items – use these as inspiration for your own creative journey.

NATURAL DYEING

Natural dyes are extracted from natural sources, such as plants, minerals and insects. Plants provide the largest range of natural colours, from leaves, flowers, roots, berries, nuts, seeds, wood and bark, and from fungi and lichen. Mineral dyes use pigments from earth and rocks, such as ochre and umber. Insect dyes are made from cochineal, kermes and lac insects. These sources, being naturally of the earth, can be inherently full of vitamins, minerals and herbal qualities.

Natural dyes can be used with textiles – 'in the fleece', the yarn, the cloth or the finished sewn piece. It can also be applied directly onto paper surfaces or onto any other natural material, such as shells, leather, wood or ceramics. The colour achieved has lustre and depth because it is made up of many particles of varying colours – unlike a synthetic pantone dye colour, which is made of only one or two single pigments and appears flat. Also, because natural dyes contain so many colour particles, different dye colours complement each other rather than creating the jarring effect that you can sometimes get with synthetic dyes.

It feels warming to the soul to know and feel that the materials you use to create beautiful things are in themselves full of beauty, safe to use and might even nourish the skin, body and wider environment.

HISTORY OF NATURAL DYEING

Deriving colour from natural resources is believed to have developed simultaneously around the world from as far back as the Neolithic period, which was roughly from 10,000 BC. Evidence from this period shows that natural pigments from minerals were used to paint cave walls, shells, stones, hides and feathers. However, paints sit on the surface, so are different from dyes, which actually bond with the fibre. It is difficult to trace the historical use of natural dyes because of the lack of written records and the nature of dyed materials, which erode and decay quickly unless they are very well preserved – such as in the mummification techniques of ancient burial tombs.

The earliest written records of dyeing date back to China in 2600 BC, with recipes for red, black and yellow dyes. Examples of natural-dyed textiles have been found preserved in the tomb of Tutankhamen and in pre-Incan burial tombs. There are references to scarlet linen in the Bible, and to dyed robes in the writings of Alexander the Great and the great writers Dioscorides, Pliny the Elder and Herodotus.

In the Middle Ages, those with plant knowledge – healers, herbalists, midwives and natural dyers – are believed to have steeped their undergarments in their brews and tonics to then wear against the most sensitive parts of their skin to absorb their healing properties. Unfortunately many of these wise people were denounced as witches and were executed, but a very few went into hiding and continued to pass their skills onto later generations, keeping the plant knowledge alive until it could safely be practised again.

Across the globe through history, natural dyes and fibres have been characteristic of the local bio-region. The natural resources available help to shape the potential for colour, the ways in which fibre is manipulated, and the tools and methods with which the colour is applied. Some places are fortunate to have plants that provide exciting colours, such as the bright pinks and red of sappanwood in India, the deep rare blues of indigo from the tropics, vivid pinks of cochineal from Mexico, and the revered Tyrian purple of the ancient Phoenicians from the west Mediterranean.

Some dyes were so rare and valuable that they were reserved solely for the enjoyment of royalty, as a status symbol. Tyrian purple is a good example of this: it was worth its weight in gold, due to the laborious task of crushing thousands of sea snails to capture their purple secretions, so its brilliant purple adorned only the cloaks of kings and priests.

In Europe, the range of colours tended towards softer hues: gentle pinks, yellows, earthy oranges and browns, and light greens. They are delicate and beautiful in their own right, sitting well with the soft landscape and natural colours of the flora and fauna.

The development of colour palettes was also connected to the discovery of new mordants to help fix colours. Alum and iron were used as mordants in ancient Egypt and India, while medieval dyers are believed to have used iron, copper, alum and tin for their dye baths. In places where access to such metals was limited, plant-based mordants such as rhubarb, club moss or oak gall were used. Other possibilities were seawater, soymilk, staghorn sumac, juniper needles, symplocos, stale urine or naturally iron-rich mud.

As more trade routes opened up around the world, with tropical dye materials travelling via camel back from China and aboard sea vessels from the Americas, the use of brighter dyes became popular with the wealthiest European families who could afford the expense of the costly imports. Dye materials were often considered the perfect shipping commodity: they were rare, high value, low in volume, and long lasting so could survive long journeys. By the 18th century, British colonialism saw the development of large-scale operations to meet the demands of a growing consumer culture, while the Industrial Revolution taking place in Europe led to mass production.

But as machines replaced people in textile and paper factories, standards for dye colour and colour fastness became more demanding. Chemists began to find ways of extracting isolated colour particles from dyes to make more intensely saturated colours and eventually discovered techniques for taking colour from the by-products of the coal industry. In the mid-19th century, William Perkin was the first to develop a coal-tar derived dye, mauvine, while trying to find a form of synthetic quinine as a cure for malaria. An explosion in availability of different chemical dyes followed, which completely overtook the use of natural dyes.

Still, more traditional ways of working did survive. The Arts and Crafts movement that flourished in Britain and spread to Europe and America during 1880 to 1920 stood for the preservation of traditional craftsmanship in the fine and decorative arts. Its members were against the advancements of industry, advocating simple form, natural materials, quality and the journey of the making process itself. William Morris was one of the pioneers of this movement, and he had a preference for the pure shades offered by plants in his work, which was inspired by spending time in nature. Morris created beautifully intricate printed wallpapers and textiles, using natural dyes such as indigo, walnut, cochineal, kermes and madder. He was also deeply interested in the wellbeing of his workers, after spending a great deal of time with them at his factories, and he was concerned about the pollution caused by industry. As a result, in the late 19th century his factories were some of the very few to use traditional and more ecological techniques for dyeing and printing,

CURRENT CONTEXT

Today, the use of natural dyes is mainly limited to home and craft dyers, traditional artisans and a handful of commercial-scale units around the world. However, the detrimental environmental impact of synthetic chemicals is becoming more commonly acknowledged. The health of workers in synthetic dye industries can be compromised, with countless cases of skin diseases, respiratory problems and a range of major chronic health issues and fatalities reportedly associated. But it's not only those involved in the supply chains of these materials who are at risk of being harmed by their harsh chemical contents: consumers who wear or handle items containing certain synthetic chemicals could also be subjecting themselves to absorption of toxins into their skin.

The extensive use of water in synthetic dye manufacturing processes is problematic in itself, but more concerning is the fact that this becomes polluted. Waste water from the textile dyeing industry is notorious for being one of the most polluting in the world.

Can we afford to wait for governing bodies to clamp down on the social and environmental impact of these industries, and for the corporations responsible to become accountable for their effect on people and planet?

By bringing more awareness to the way in which things are made and reach us, we can start to think about what we want to support. We need more solutions, better alternatives for people to invest in – more independent designers and makers, using local, organic, responsibly sourced materials and low-impact production, with an awareness of environmental and social impact at the heart of their work.

A change in consumer demand could be the most effective solution for ending the damaging way in which things are made. Then we can start to move away from using synthetic dyes, textiles, paints, inks and drawing materials. In fact, it's encouraging to see a resurgence of interest in slower lifestyles and more ecological approaches to design.

Natural dyes cost the earth far less and can also be cheaper to produce than the chemical-based mass-market options. Most of the popular dye plants can be grown very easily in a garden, allotment or community growing space. There is a great charm and beauty in using, wearing and surrounding oneself in the colours of one's own environment – it's an invitation to feel more a part of and connected to the land.

FIBRESHED MODEL + BRISTOL CLOTH

All life depends on soil – animals, plants and humans. And to maintain the health of this vital matter, it's important to look at the way we grow our textiles. It's estimated that over ten thousand dyes and pigments are used within the commercial sphere, with eight thousand chemicals in them. But there is a solution to the environmental and social dangers of synthetic dye manufacturing – the Fibreshed model. This 'soil-to-soil' concept works by connecting independent regional organic fibre and dye plant producers with skilled local designers and makers, and local consumers, to regenerate regional fibre manufacturing and a resilient associated economy.

These production systems are built to be sustainable, with a view to using renewable energy-powered mills, close to farming and processing units in order to reduce transportation and its reliance on fossil fuels. In the production of the fibres and the dyes, carbon-neutral and carbon-fixing farming processes are used to rebuild the quality of the soil. By doing all this, the model considers the entire fibre-production system from soil-to-soil, so at the end of the useful lifecycle of a garment or product, it can be safely put back into the earth as biological nutrients rather than into landfill as pollutants. This means the Fibreshed model is nourishing the environment at the same time as strengthening regional economies.

In 2015 I joined forces with Emma Hague of the Bristol Textile Quarter to establish the Bristol Cloth project and produce a cloth that was locally sourced and manufactured. The Bristol Cloth is our own Fibreshed-inspired product: a 100% wool fabric making use of locally sourced materials and manufacturing processes from southwest England and

made without toxic synthetic chemicals. The naturally dyed cloth was conceived with the help of holistically managed Fernhill Farm, woven textile design studio Dash + Miller, and the Bristol Weaving Mill, the first industrial-scale loom in Bristol in 100 years.

I now run the Bristol Cloth project alone and hope to see the first Bristol Cloth meterage and products featured in stores very soon. My dream is that with a working model of what is possible, others will follow our lead to recreate a vibrant and successful organic British textile industry. With this in mind, I encourage you to explore the Fibreshed model and holistic farming in more detail.

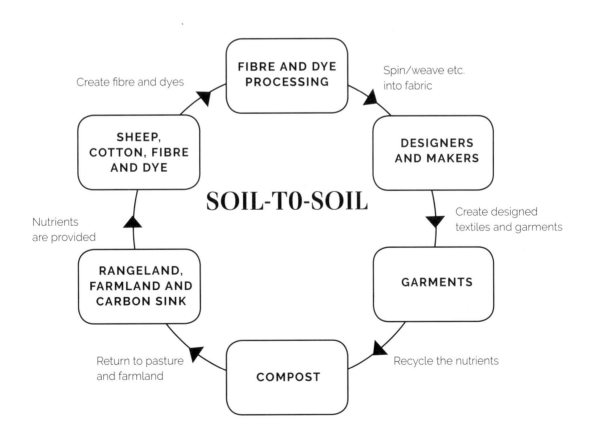

Create fibre and dyes

FIBRE AND DYE PROCESSING

Spin/weave etc. into fabric

SHEEP, COTTON, FIBRE AND DYE

SOIL-TO-SOIL

DESIGNERS AND MAKERS

Create designed textiles and garments

Nutrients are provided

RANGELAND, FARMLAND AND CARBON SINK

GARMENTS

Return to pasture and farmland

COMPOST

Recycle the nutrients

From top left: Cornflower; Pansy; Apple Tree; Echinacea

SOURCING DYE MATERIAL

There are endless sources of natural dye colours around us, from the domestic (household and garden) to public (local parks, woodlands and wildernesses). Once you start developing your eco-literacy for natural colour, you will start to see colour potential everywhere you look.

Whatever dye material you find or choose – whether that's freshly foraged plants or dried dye material from specialist suppliers – this book will guide you in turning it into a dye bath, ready to bring natural colour into your life.

HOUSE AND GARDEN

To start with, reconsider the things you throw into the bin or compost when you're cooking. Onion skins hold an incredible amount of dye colour. Discarded cabbage and kale leaves, carrot tops, ends of beetroot, and pumpkin and squash skins all yield beautiful hues. One of my all-time favourite colours is the soft dusty pink given by avocado rinds and the slightly deeper shade from the pit. You can recycle used tea bags, coffee grounds and the mulch left over from juicing various fruits and vegetables. Even leftover red wine can be used when it's no longer drinkable. This is such a great way to source colour, as you are getting an extra use out of the by-products of your cooking, and they can still go into the compost afterwards to nourish the land.

If you're lucky enough to have a garden or allotment, then you have an almost limitless opportunity for growing colour. Many herbs, such as rosemary, mint, sage and thyme, give good strong colours. They are often pretty hardy plants too, which carry on growing throughout the colder months of year and so offer an ongoing source of colour. Along with a selection of garden vegetables and herbs, you can also grow various flowers such as roses, daffodils, tulips and hollyhocks for brighter shades and for using with bundle-dyeing and hapazome techniques. You can also buy traditional dye plant seeds and rhizomes (from certified organic sources), such as madder, weld and even indigo, to grow in your garden. For more ideas, see the following page.

FARM AND WILDERNESS

If you live near any farms, find out what grows in them and if the farmer would be happy to let you take away any waste produce or invasive weeds. Dock plants are big nuisance to farmers and most would welcome the opportunity to be relieved of them. Things such as walnut husks are discarded once the walnuts have been removed, and can be recycled for making the most wonderful shades of brown and black.

If you don't have access to a garden or farm, look around at your local landscape. There are endless plants that have colour potential in the wild and natural spaces around us. Where I live, there are hedgerow plants that grow abundantly – such as nettles, blackberries, and apple trees – and other species that are commonly found in woodland, such as bracken and pine. Meadows and lawns are often dotted with outcrops of yarrow, dock and dandelion. Even waste ground can be a great place for finding certain plants and herbs that have made it their home.

When collecting leaves and flowers, use those that have naturally fallen to the ground. If you do take cuttings from the plant, try not to overharvest from one part of the plant. Take leaves/flowers from every third leaf/flower on the stem, or from every third plant. And only take from healthy plants which can then easily regenerate. You can also collect seeds or take cuttings to propagate from local wild plants.

Always ask the landowner for permission before you forage for any plants, even if it is a public space.

ONLINE

For any other types of dye that you cannot grow or source locally, you can go to responsible online suppliers of sustainable natural dyes. These come as dried dye materials including wood chips, powders or extract powders. For more on this, see p53.

TIPS ON GROWING
YOUR OWN DYE GARDEN

Tansy

Each season brings with it a new palette of colours, from different parts of a plant, or from entirely different plants. Depending on where your are in the world, your choice of plants will be directed by those that are native or will grow well in the soil and climate.

To maximise their usage, consider using plants that offer a range of properties within themselves: herbs that heal and give colour, fruit and vegetables that offer nutrition as well as pigments. Focus on planting a good number of self-propagating perennial varieties, which do not need replanting each year. And try growing plants that grow back quickly when cut, such as kale and mint. Also consider having a patch of nettles – they are wonderful at quickly regenerating and seem to thrive when cut back every now and then. They also offer excellent nitrogen fixing qualities to enrich your soil. You can also grow natural ingredients for mordants, such as rhubarb, borage or a walnut tree.

It's good to have a mixture of annuals, with a thought to what colours will be available through each season of the plant's growth cycle. Consider which part of the plant you will use to extract colour. Can you use the leaves, fruit and nuts, rather than having to dig up the whole plant for its roots? If so, you have a renewable resource at your fingertips. When you're ready to use your plant, consider where the energy of the plant is during different times of the year. In the cooler months, the energy will be stored in the roots, then it moves up into new leaves. When seeding, the energy and strong colour will be in the seeds, and once these dry and fall off, the energy cycles back down into the roots. Go to where the energy of the plant is, for its richest colour source.

Aim for a collection of plants that will give you a rainbow of colours to choose from. In temperate climates, you can start by using woad for blue, madder for rich reds, dock and dandelion root for mustard yellows, hollyhocks for dark red, sunflowers for their purple-producing seeds, onions for orange, comfrey for green and meadowsweet for black. Indigo, madder and weld are the traditional three primary colours used to attain a wider range of colours, so consider planting these from seed.

THE LANGUAGE OF DYEING

Acid (acidic) and Alkali (alkaline) This refers to substances that sit on the pH-scale. If a substance has a pH level 1–4 it is acidic, if the pH level is 5–7 it is neutral; 8–11 is alkaline. You can test the pH level of a substance using litmus paper.

Alum In this book, alum refers to potassium aluminium sulphate. It is a non-toxic metallic compound which can be used as a mordant to help fix dyes to fibres.

Curing A curing process is often used to help colour set into fibre. To cure a fibre that has been dyed, hang it somewhere dry, out of direct sunlight. Leave it to air dry and cure for a period of time, from several days to weeks, before washing. The longer you leave it, the better the setting results.

Disposal of dyes When working with non-toxic natural dyes in small quantities, you can dispose of remaining dye bath solutions by diluting them with water and flushing them into the sewage system/down the drain. In some cases, you can use the remaining dye bath as feed for certain plants (see 'Disposal of mordants and modifiers'). Those working with larger quantities should use a professional water filtration system to clean their dye water before it goes into the sewage system/down the drain.

Disposal of mordants and modifiers When working with non-toxic mordants (alum, iron and tannin) and modifiers in small quantities, you can dispose of them by diluting with plenty of water and then flushing them into the sewage system/down the drain. Alum and iron mordants can also be poured into the soil near the roots of acid-loving plants such as heather, laburnum, blue spruce and magnolia. If doing so, dilute with lots of water first and pour into different spots around your garden, over a course of time, so as not to effect the pH balance of the soil or damage the plants.

Dye bath A solution of dye pigments suspended in water which is used to dye fibres.

Dye colour To check a dye bath has a deep enough colour, dip a spoon into the bowl: if it disappears and you can't see it under the surface, you have lots of colour.

Dye pot A non-reactive vessel used to contain a dye bath. In this book, it is often referred to simply as a 'pot'.

Dye material The material used for dyeing, such as plant material (leaf, flower, root, berry, nut, bark), or food waste. This can be fresh or dry, whole or chips/shavings. It covers dye powder and extract powder.

Extract powder A dye powder that is made up of dye particles that have been isolated and extracted from the original dye material – it is much stronger than standard dye powder. It is sometimes referred to as 'dye extract powder'.

Fastness (light, colour, rub, wash) A quality of being fixed and a measure of the resistance of a material or dye to fading, caused by exposure to light, rubbing, wear, washing or age.

Fibre In this book, fibre refers to textiles and paper, and their natural substance – eg animal fibres for textiles such as silk and alpaca, or plant fibres for textiles such as hemp and cotton. The term 'fabric' is also used throughout the project pages, which is interchangeable with 'cloth'.

Modify/modifier Modifiers are solutions used to change the colour of dye, to give a wider range of colours. Dyes are modified to give different colour results.

Mordant A solution that is used to help dyes bond with fibre for more colourfast results. It also affects the colour outcomes of the dye. It can be used before (pre-mordant), during or after (post-mordant/after-mordant) the dye process. The best results are often obtained from pre-mordanting.

Non-reactive Material for dye pot and equipment that will not react with dyes, such as stainless steel, glass and ceramic. As opposed to reactive materials, such as iron, tin and copper, which can leach into solutions and cause changes in colour.

Overdye To dye fibre that has already been dyed, therefore adding another layer of dye colour on top, which may alter the overall shade of the fibre.

Layer dye Some dyes work better when colour is built up in layers, by dyeing the fibre once, and then again. This is in contrast to using more dye material in a dye bath. Layer dyeing can give longer-lasting and more reliable results.

pH A numeric scale used to determine the acidity or alkalinity of a water soluble substance.

pH-neutral soap A mild soap with a neutral pH level, which is suitable for sensitive skin. Most soaps have an alkaline pH level which can damage skin/fibre and also affect delicate natural dyes and alter colours. It's best practice to use pH-neutral soaps for all natural dyeing processes and to care for naturally dyed fibres, to preserve and lengthen the life of their colours. I like to use Dr Bronner's organic baby unscented liquid soap.

Pre-wet/pre-wetting Before using any textiles (cloth, yarn or fleece) for any natural dyeing process, including mordanting, dyeing and modifying, you should always ensure your fibre is thoroughly wetted. This ensures the fibre particles are open, porous and most able to receive dye/mordant/modifier solutions consistently all over. Do this by soaking it in clean water, ideally for 8-12 hours, or at the very least 1 hour. For full instructions, see p30.

Sampling Always test a scrap piece of your fibre in the mordant, dye bath or modifier solution in order to check you have the correct solutions to create your desired colour outcomes.

Scour Cloth, yarn, fleece (all fibre except paper, in this book) should always be scoured prior to any part of the dye process in order to remove dirt, grease, starches or dust and ultimately achieve good, clear and consistent colours. For full instructions, see p30.

Safety Precautions should always be followed when handling mordant, dye and modifier materials. Use protective goggles to cover eyes, gloves for hands and dust mask for airways, and work in a well-ventilated area. Do not put any materials in your mouth and keep away from children and animals. Always supervise children.

Sustainable Using methods that allow biological systems to remain diverse and healthy, avoiding depletion or permanent damage of natural resources or the environment.

Water This book offers guidelines for the amount of water to use, but no exact measures. This is because the amount of water you need will depend on the size of the fibre you are dyeing and the dye pot you are using. You always need to use enough clean water to allow your fibre to move freely. Make sure there is space at the top of the dye pot to allow the dye bath to simmer, boil or be stirred. If at any time in the process you don't have enough water, top up with more clean water at a similar temperature. This won't dilute the dye colour – the same amount of colour remains in the water. Keep an eye on water to maintain suitable levels throughout all processes. The temperature of the water isn't too important, but it's what's comfortable for your hands. There are times when boiling water is necessary, and this has been stated throughout.

Weighing fibre/fabric Many of the dye recipes will require you to weigh the fibre. Always do this after it has been washed and scoured and left to dry – you'd be surprised how much dirt will be washed away and how much that dirt weighed.

Wood chips Some wood dyes, such as logwood and sappanwood, can be bought as wood chips. These are made from cutting or chipping larger parts of the wood.

CHOOSING THE
RIGHT FIBRES

Before starting, consider the most suitable fibre (textile/fabric) for your project. Natural fibres, in their unbleached and undyed state, are the first choice for natural dyeing practices.

Many fibres are bleached to give a pure white colour in place of their natural grey or beige. This renders the natural dying process somewhat obsolete, so try to buy unbleached and undyed fibres to work with. Their natural colour provides a good base on which to build and enrich your dye colours. Additionally, try to choose organically grown and sustainable varieties. I've listed some of my favourite suppliers on p185.

Generally, there are two groups of fibres – animal (protein) fibres, or plant (cellulose) fibres. Depending on which of the two groups the fabric belongs to, the way in which it should be treated and how it responds to the dye process will differ. The following pages will give you an overview of the variety of fibres available, and how they pair with various mordants.

A note on sustainable fibres

Using sustainable fibres is key in any environmentally conscious process. Most sustainable fibres come with pros and cons – it's hard to find one that is 100% environmentally and socially positive. Look at the full lifecycle, from the soil it is grown in to the effect it will have when it goes back into the earth at the end of its lifecycle. From this informed position you can decide which fibres suit your own priorities.

Many 'eco-fibres', such as bamboo, rayon, viscose and tencel, are made from plant fibres – but they require intensive chemical processing to turn them into fabric. For this reason I choose to avoid them entirely. Petroleum-based synthetic fibres, such as polyester, are derived from oil and do not biodegrade. And, when laundered, acrylic fabrics have been found to release millions of micro-plastic particles into the water systems, posing an environmental threat to marine wildlife, as well as entering the food chain. Recycled fibres are made from scraps of textile from factories or post-consumer use, which are spun into thread for making new fabrics. Despite the waste reduction, they can contain synthetic fibres or chemicals so pose the same issues as other synthetic fibres.

Plant fibres

```
COTTON
LINEN
HEMP
RAMIE
NETTLE
```

Plant fibres will require more processing than animal fibres in order to achieve the same intensity of colour when dyed. The colours will often appear pale unless a mordant is used to help fix the dye, as plant fibres are fairly stubborn at receiving colour. In a sense, we use a mordant to make them act more like animal fibres, and so take up the colour better.

Plant fibres are much more resilient than animal fibres when it comes to temperature changes and extremes – they can generally be boiled without damage, and going from hot to cold or vice versa will not have such dramatic effects.

A note on recycled paper
Paper can be made from all kinds of plant fibres, from wood, banana and mango plants to cotton and mushrooms. You can look for eco-paper suppliers – in the UK there is a company producing paper made with the by-product of corn farming. Recycled paper is usually made from post-consumer waste paper, which means that it is likely to contain varying levels of synthetic pigments and solvents, although it is possible to find recycled paper that has not undergone further chemical bleaching, processing or colouring. Ideally buy your paper from a local mill. Or look for Khadi paper, which is made from post-consumer cotton in India, and has a beautiful soft texture to it. Do note, it is generally made with bleached cotton and may be mixed with additional synthetic materials.

SUSTAINABLE PLANT FIBRES
Organic cotton This uses fewer chemical pesticides and fertilisers than standard cotton, although still requires vast amounts of water for growing and processing. If it's grown in rainy countries this is less of a problem, but many producers are in drought-prone areas and rely on mains water or river water, which then impacts local communities. Sadly, only about 1% of global cotton production uses organic systems.

Linen Made from the flax plant, which requires minimal fertilisers for growing and less pesticide control than cotton. Linen is one of the strongest fibres: it is breathable, highly absorbent and takes dye well compared to other plant fibres.

Hemp A quick-growing bast-fibre plant that provides a fast turnover of crop, and easily provides 2–3 times more fibre per acre than cotton. It doesn't require the use of herbicides or pesticides because it is naturally pest-tolerant. And it enriches the soil by fixing nutrients back into it. As a fabric, hemp is breathable, warm, moisture wicking, anti-bacterial and durable.

Ramie A perennial plant that has been cultivated for its fibre for thousands of years. Native to eastern Asia and belonging to the same family as the nettle, its strong bast fibre reaches very long lengths, making it ideal to spin for textiles. Ramie grows quickly and well without the use of chemical herbicides and pesticides. The task of retting – to remove the fibre from the plant and process it – is specialist and requires hard manual work, which makes it expensive to produce. When produced by hand ramie is chemical free, but it can also be produced industrially, in which case it's chemically intensive. Ramie is a lustrous fabric, similar to silk, although much stronger.

Nettle This grows abundantly with low maintenance and minimal water in most bio-regions. Nettles grow in the poorest-quality soil and fix nitrogen and other nutrients back into it; no herbicides or pesticides are required. Nettle fabric is a soft and lustrous fibre.

Animal fibres

```
WOOL
SILK
ALPACA
MOHAIR
```

These fibres tend to take up dye colours and hold on to them much more successfully than plant fibres and can often be used without a mordant.

However, they can be delicate, and need to be treated very gently when processing. Use cold or low-temperature dyeing techniques so as not to disrupt the quality of the fibres. Silk can lose its sheen when a high heat is applied, while wool is quick to shrink if used with hot temperatures.

It's also important not to shock the animal fibres by taking them from one extreme temperature to another. Instead, let temperature changes happen gradually, allowing a dye bath to cool naturally before removing the fibres and washing them in cool water. Similarly, put cold-washed fibres into a cold dye bath and increase the temperature slowly.

SUSTAINABLE ANIMAL FIBRES

Wool Organic wool is available from a limited number of farmers. In the UK, organic wool comes from sheep that are only fed 100% organic grains and that graze on certified organic land, and chemical dips and antibiotics are not used. Ideally organic sheep are grazed in rotation with cattle, allowing both animals access to different grasses, which provide wider nutritional value.

Peace silk A lustrous fabric, made from the cocoons of silk worms. For conventional silk the worm is killed by boiling the cocoon, but peace silk, or ahimsa silk, allows the worm to live and hatch out as a moth. This means that the single continuous thread of the cocoon is broken into several pieces, where the creature has eaten its way out. As a consequence, the fibre requires extra work to spin and therefore is more expensive, although the result is as good as other silk.

Alpaca Made from the fleece of the alpaca, a South American camelid that looks similar to a small llama. Alpaca wool is softer than sheep wool, as well as being free of lanolin, which makes it hypoallergenic. Alpacas are usually grazed on mountainsides, where they roam freely, and generally require no pesticides or antibiotic treatment, so their wool is often naturally organic.

Mohair This comes from the mohair goat. It's silky and strong, with natural flame retardancy and elasticity, and it doesn't felt or crease. The majority of commercial mohair comes from South Africa and the USA. Make sure you source it from small-scale farms using sustainable practices, such as rotational grazing (which encourages soil health), and hand blade-shearing, to improve animal welfare.

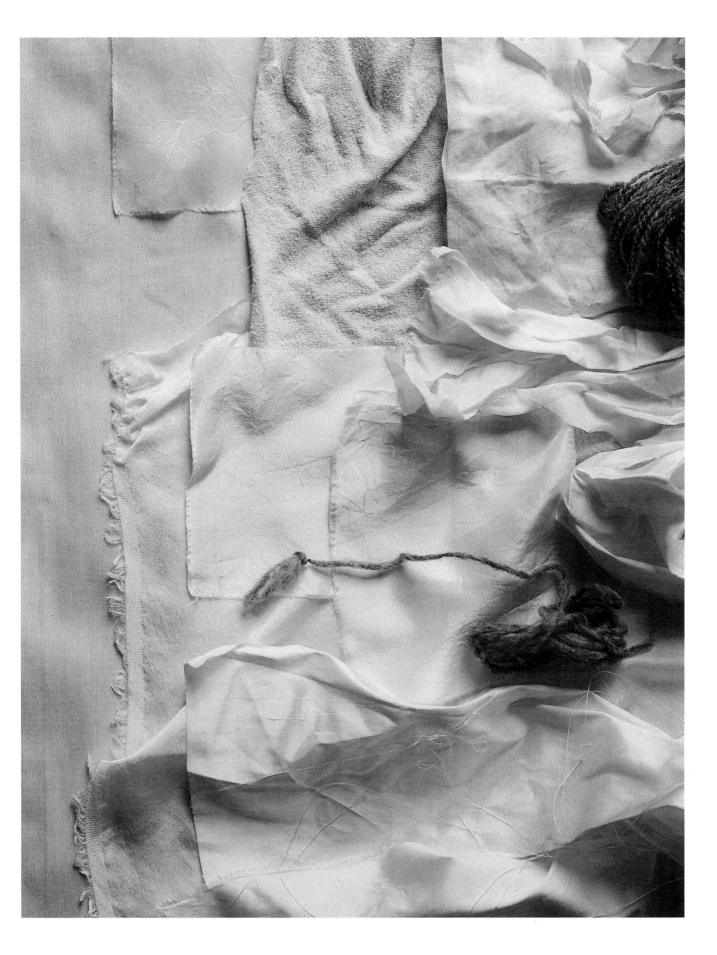

WASHING AND SCOURING

Before using fibres for dyeing or printing you need to prepare them properly, so that no dust, grease, starch or any kind of dirt is hiding within them, which might disrupt the quality of the dye results.

1 First, put the fibre through a 40°C (104°F) wash in the washing machine, or wash by hand if using fibres that are too delicate for machine washing.

2 To scour the fibre, put it straight from the wash – in its damp state – into a large non-reactive pot filled with water. It should be big enough for the fibre to move around freely in. It's important not to overload the pot, as the dirt needs to be able to easily escape from the folds of the fibre.

3 Add an ecological soap, which is safe to dispose of and non-irritating to the skin. You'll need a similar amount of soap as you might for your normal laundry load.

4 If using delicate animal fibres such as silk, wool or cashmere, bring the water to a gentle simmer and keep it there for an hour, stirring regularly. Then turn off the heat and leave the fibre to cool in the water.

5 If using sturdier plant fibres such as linen or cotton, bring the water to the boil, and continue to boil for an hour, stirring regularly. Then turn off the heat and leave the fibres to cool in the water.

6 Once everything has cooled, tip away the dirty, soapy water and replace it with clean water to rinse the fibres in by hand. You may need to repeat this two or three times, until the water appears clear of soap suds and dirt.

You can use the fibres right away, in their damp state. If you don't need them immediately, hang them out to air dry and then store them in sealed bags or boxes to protect them from moths, dust and dirt until you are ready to use them.

WEIGHING FIBRE

Many of the dye recipes will require you to weigh the fibre. Always do this after it has been washed and scoured and left to dry – you'd be surprised how much dirt will be washed away and how much that dirt weighed.

PRE-WETTING

Fibres need to be pre-wetted before going into the dye bath. This allows them to be used in a damp state, so the particles which make up the fibre are expanded, open and therefore porous, making them more able to receive the solution in which they are submerged. This means they can take up consistent, all-over dye, mordant or modifier.

To pre-wet a fibre, place it in a large pot of water and allow it to soak for at least one hour, or for better results 8–12 hours/overnight. The longer you leave it, the better the outcome.

MORDANTING/PRE-WETTING

After mordanting, fibres can be washed, rinsed and wrung to remove excess water. And then in their damp state, they can be added into the dye bath – no need for further pre-wetting.

However, if the mordanted fibre has been allowed to air dry (perhaps for use later), then it will need to be pre-wetted. When you're ready to dye, pre-wet the fibre following the instructions above, and use in its damp state.

MORDANTS

Most dyes require a fixative, which dyers call a mordant, to help the colours chemically bond with the fibres. The word 'mordant' comes from the Latin word *mordere*, which means 'to bite': the mordant allows the colour to bite into the fibre so it is resistant (fast) to light, washing or rubbing.

Mordanting can be done before, during or after the dyeing process. I recommend 'pre-mordanting' before dyeing for the most reliable and consistent results (except for iron, which is better as an after-mordant). The type of fibre will dictate the kind of mordant you need to use – animal fibres require different mordants to plant fibres.

Mordants also impact the colour of the dye. On the chart on p66–67 you can see the difference in dye colour results when a mineral-based mordant is used, compared to when a plant-based mordant is used, this is on both animal and plant fibres.

Plant-based mordants are preferable to mineral-based mordants as they are natural, renewable resources, and generally safer to dispose of after use. The drawback of using plant-based mordants is that they tend to leave a slight beige or yellow tint on fabric prior to dyeing, which can affect the colour outcomes of the dye if you are aiming for pale shades – it can often mean deeper hues, which shouldn't be an issue if you are after rich, deep shades. However, if you are aiming for a light, pale or bright colour – such as bubblegum pink or pastel yellow – you may find it hard to achieve. The colour chart (p66–67) highlights that rich and beautifully muted colours can be achieved with plant-based mordants.

Storing mordants

See p20 for how to dispose of a mordant. Note that mordant baths can be reserved as a base for future mordant making. Store them in lidded buckets or airtight jars in a cool, dark, dry place. To use, top up the remaining mordant with the correct quantity of ingredients based on the weight of your fabric.

The rhubarb mordant (p32) can be kept up to 6 months. The alum and cream of tartar mordant (p35) can be kept indefinitely. The oak gall mordant (p37) can also be stored for years. If anything starts to smell, you may prefer to dispose of it.

PLANT-BASED MORDANTS

Plant fibres can be mordanted with a plant-based mordant such as tannic acid, which can easily be extracted from oak galls (this is the most traditional and effective in the UK), as well as oak bark, chestnuts, acorns, walnuts and other nuts and barks.

Animal fibres can be mordanted with a plant-based mordant such as oxalic acid, which is extracted from rhubarb leaf (also the most traditional and commonly used in the UK), as well as staghorn sumac, borage and certain seaweeds.

When considering employing a more sustainable practice, it is good to look at which plant-based mordants you have access to in your local environment, before defaulting to mineral-based mordants, which are often either synthetically produced or finite resources (except for homemade iron water, see p43). In any case, it is best to avoid using most heavy metals as they are considered toxic, and to follow safety precautions when processing any plant mordants which might be toxic, too.

MINERAL-BASED MORDANTS

These days mineral-based mordants tend to be synthetically produced versions of the natural mineral, but at least this means that they don't use finite resources.

I only work with iron and alum (potassium aluminium sulphate), as mineral mordants. It's best to avoid using any heavy metals that are considered toxic (such as copper or tin). Alum is considered a non-toxic light metal and iron is a heavy metal which is considered safe to use in small quantities. When used properly, with the correct quantities, alum is fully absorbed into fibres so after use there should be none left in the water that might get flushed down the drain. However, you should always dispose of remaining mordant responsibly (see p20).

Alum can be used with both animal and plant fibres but it requires an assistant – or 'assist' – to help the fibres absorb it completely. For plant fibres the assist is soda ash. For animal fibres, cream of tartar is used.

Mordants for animal fibres

PLANT-BASED MORDANT
RHUBARB LEAF

Rhubarb is a perennial plant that regrows each year without the need for replanting. Although the raw leaf is high in oxalic acid, which is toxic, the acid is broken down with heat and therefore non-toxic after it has been extracted with heat and used for mordanting. It can simply be dug into the ground or put on the compost heap after use.

Rhubarb leaf does leave a beige-yellow colour on fabrics when used as a mordant, and this has an effect on the outcomes if you are trying to achieve a pale shade: colours may seem a little murky compared to those mordanted with a mineral-based mordant. They are beautiful colours nonetheless.

Plant-based mordant recipe

As this mordant is based on rhubarb leaf (oxalic acid), it's important to work with it in a well-ventilated area, as the fumes are toxic. Protect your hands with gloves and wear a dust mask and eye protectors when working close to the pot.

Fibre (washed, scoured and dry)
Rhubarb leaves
Scales
3 large pots, with lids
Strainer
Long-handled spoon
pH-neutral soap

1 Weigh the fibre after it has been washed, scoured and dried. Use 200% of the weight of the fibre in rhubarb leaf. For example, for 100g (3½oz) of fibre, use 200g (7oz) of rhubarb leaf. You should weigh the fibre and calculate the correct weight of rhubarb to use before you begin preparing the mordant.

2 Place the fibre in a large pot of water and allow it to soak for at least 1 hour, or ideally 8–12 hours/overnight, so that the fibre is pre-wetted.

3 Wash the leaves and chop them up very small so that they are shredded. Put them into another large pot, which should be big enough for them to be completely covered with water.

4 Cover the leaves with boiling water. Bring the water to a simmer, cover with a lid and simmer for one hour.

5 After one hour, turn off the heat and leave the pot to cool Once the solution has cooled, strain out the plant material, reserving the liquid in another large pot with a lid. The pot should be big enough to hold the fibre you want to mordant, and you need to make sure there is enough liquid for the fibre to move around freely so that the mordant can reach all of it consistently. Top up with more warm water if there isn't enough.

6 Add the pre-wetted fibre to the mordant solution. Bring the solution to a simmer, cover with a lid, and simmer for 1 hour.

7 Stir gently and occasionally with a long-handled spoon. Be sure to tease out any air bubbles trapped under the fibre, as this can make it rise above the surface of the liquid where the mordant cannot reach it properly. Moving the fibre also helps to separate any areas that have been touching, or touching the side of the pot, where the mordant may not be able to reach them.

8 Turn off the heat and allow everything to cool. Once cooled, move the fibre from the solution. Gently wring out excess liquid.

9 Rinse the fibre with cool water, wash it with pH-neutral soap and cool/lukewarm water, then rinse it again to remove the soap.

10 Use the fibre in its damp state and add it to your dye bath. Or hang out the fibre to air dry somewhere warm and dry, out of direct sunlight, for later use.

MINERAL-BASED MORDANT
ALUM AND CREAM OF TARTAR

Alum (potassium aluminium sulphate) helps to improve the colourfastness of dyes, so they are less likely to fade from light and washing. It also helps to brighten colour tones. It is considered non-toxic in small quantities, so it is safe to use, but it should not be inhaled, ingested or come into contact with skin as it can cause irritation. You can buy it online or from Asian or South American food stores.

It is important to use the exact quantities of alum required for the weight of your fibre, so that it is all absorbed by the fibre and not wasted.

Cream of tartar is a synthetic compound that is considered safe enough to use as a food additive. It acts as an assist to help the uptake of the alum by the fibre.

Mineral-based mordant recipe

This mordant is based on alum and cream of tartar. Always work in a well-ventilated area and wear gloves, dust mask and eye protectors when working with alum-based mordants.

Fibre (washed, scoured and dry)
Scales
Alum
Cream of tartar
2 large pots, with lids
Measuring spoons
Heatproof jar
Long-handled spoon
Small lid or plate (optional)
pH-neutral soap

1 Weigh the fibre after it has been washed, scoured and dried. Use 8% of the weight of the fibre in alum, and 7% of the weight of the fibre in cream of tartar. You should weigh the fibre and calculate the correct weight of alum and cream of tartar to use before you begin preparing the mordant.

2 Place the fibre in a large pot of water and allow it to soak for at least one hour, or ideally 8–12 hours/overnight, so that the fibre is pre-wetted.

3 Fill a pot with room-temperature water. The pot should be large enough to contain the fibre you want to mordant and allow enough water for it to be covered and move around freely.

4 Measure out the cream of tartar into a heatproof jar and add enough boiling water for it to dissolve completely when stirred. Then add this to the pot of water, stirring with a long-handled spoon to mix it in.

5 Measure out the alum into the heatproof jar and add enough boiling water for it to dissolve completely when stirred. Then add this to the pot of water, again stirring with a long-handled spoon to mix it in.

6 Add the pre-wetted fibre to the mordant solution. Bring the solution to a simmer, cover with a lid and simmer for one hour.

7 Stir gently and occasionally with a long-handled spoon. Be sure to tease out any air bubbles trapped under the fibre, as this can make it rise above the surface of the liquid where the mordant cannot reach it properly. Moving the fibre also helps to separate any areas that have been touching, or touching the side of the pot, where the mordant may not be able to reach them.

8 Turn off the heat and allow the fibre to cool in the pot overnight. Then remove the fibre from the pot and gently wring out any excess liquid.

9 Rinse the fibre with cool water, wash with pH-neutral soap and cool/lukewarm water, then rinse again to remove the soap.

10 Use the fibre in its damp state and add it to your dye bath. Or hang out the fibre to air dry somewhere warm and dry, out of direct sunlight, for later use.

Mordants for plant fibres

PLANT-BASED MORDANT
OAK GALL

A simple one-step method for mordanting plant fibres is to use tannic acid extracted from oak galls. Oak galls are small spherical growths that form on oak trees when the gall wasp lays its eggs in the buds of the tree. The tree reacts by growing tissue around the egg, which protects it until it hatches out, leaving behind an escape hole. You should look for this hole when harvesting to ensure that the oak galls you pick do not still have a creature inside them. Usually the end of the summer is a good time to harvest, or when leaves have fallen off the tree later in the year and the galls are easier to spot. You can also easily buy online whole galls or oak gall extract powder for mordanting. I've used the extract powder in this recipe.

Because of their particularly high tannin content, oak galls are an excellent plant-based mordant for plant fibres. But remember they can leave a beige hue on the fabric.

One-step plant-based mordant recipe

This mordant is based on oak gall (tannic acid). Wear gloves when making this mordant to avoid any irritation.

Fibre (washed, scoured and dry)
Scales
2 large pots
Oak gall extract powder
Jar
Long-handled spoon
pH-neutral soap

1 You will need 1 tsp of oak gall extract powder for every 100g (3½oz) of fibre weight after it's been washed, scoured and dried. You should weigh the fibre and calculate the correct weight of gall to use before you begin preparing the mordant.

2 Place the fibre in a large pot of water and allow it to soak for at least 1 hour, or ideally 8–12 hours/overnight, so that the fibre is pre-wetted.

3 Meanwhile, place the required amount of oak gall powder in a jar and add enough hot water to make a paste. Stir in more hot water to make a solution, allowing the powder to dissolve in the water.

4 Fill a large pot with water; the pot should be big enough for the fibre to be covered with water, with space for it to move around freely.

5 Pour the oak gall mordant solution into the pot and stir it in with a long-handled spoon. Bring to a simmer and simmer for one hour. Turn off the heat and allow the pot to cool to a lukewarm temperature.

6 Take the pre-wetted fibre out of the soaking water, and gently wring out any excess water. Place the fibre in the mordant solution and leave to soak for 8–12 hours, stirring occasionally so that the fibre absorbs the mordant consistently all over.

7 Remove the fibre from the solution and gently wring out any excess liquid. Rinse the fibre in lukewarm or cool water, then gently wash it with pH-neutral soap and rinse it again with water to remove the soap.

8 Use the fibre in its damp state and add it to your dye bath. Or hang out the fibre to air dry somewhere warm and dry, out of direct sunlight, for later use.

MINERAL-BASED MORDANT
OAK GALL WITH ALUM AND SODA ASH

A two-step method is the most effective option for saturated, deep and strong, long-lasting dye results on plant-based fibres. Alum, with soda ash as an assist, together help the uptake of dyes, brighten colours and ensure they last longer. You need to follow the oak gall mordant recipe first (see p37), then undertake a second mordanting.

Soda ash (sodium carbonate) was originally obtained from the ashes of certain plants and seaweed. It is now available as a synthetically produced mineral, made from limestone and salt. While it has many purposes, including being used in baking, eye protectors, gloves and a dust mask should be worn when handling it, as the dust can be an irritant.

For more on alum (aluminium potassium sulphate) see p35. Do note, it should not be inhaled or ingested, or come into contact with skin as it can cause irritation.

Two-step mineral-based mordant recipe

This mordant is based on oak gall (tannic acid) plus alum and soda ash. When working with alum and soda ash mordants, always work in a well-ventilated area and wear gloves, dust mask and eye protection.

Fibre, prepared with the one-step plant-based recipe
(see p37)
Alum
Heatproof jar
Soda ash
Scales
2 large pots, with lids
Long-handled spoon
pH-neutral soap

1 Weigh the fibre after it has been washed, scoured and dried. You will need 20% of the fibre's weight in alum, and 6% of its weight in soda ash. For example, for 100g (3½oz) fibre, you'll need 20g (½oz) alum and 6g (⅛oz) soda ash. You should weigh the fibre and calculate the correct weight of gall and soda ash to use before you begin preparing the mordant.

2 Follow all the steps of the one-step plant-based mordant, and once the fibre is hanging to dry, make the alum mordant.

3 Choose a pot that is large enough to allow the fibre to be covered with water and with space for it to move around easily. Half-fill the pot with water.

4 Measure out the alum based on the ratio outlined above. Add it to a heatproof jar and add enough boiling water for it to dissolve. Then add this to the pot of water.

5 Measure out the soda ash based on the ratio outlined above, and add it to the pot of water.

6 Bring the water to a simmer, stirring to dissolve soda ash thoroughly. Add more water so that there will be a sufficient amount to cover the fibres, and stir well to mix it.

7 Add the fibre, which will still be damp if you are at the end of the one-step mordanting process. If you have broken up the process and the fibre is now dry, you'll need to pre-wet it first: place it in a large pot of water and allow it to soak for at least 1 hour, or ideally 8–12 hours/overnight.

8 Heat to a simmer. Once at a simmering point, turn off the heat and leave to soak for 8 hours, stirring occasionally so that the fibre absorbs the mordant consistently all over.

9 Take the fibre out of the pot and gently wring out any excess liquid. Rinse the fibre with lukewarm or cool water, gently wash it with pH-neutral soap, then rinse it again to remove the soap.

10 Use the fibre in its damp state and add it to your dye bath. Or hang out the fibre to air dry somewhere warm and dry, out of direct sunlight, for later use.

MODIFIERS

After you've mordanted and dyed the fibre, you can extend the range of dye colours further by using modifiers to shift them to different tones, or sometimes change them to entirely different colours altogether.

Adding an acidic or alkaline modifier can change the pH-level of a dye bath. Or you can create a modifier bath in a separate bowl, which the dyed fabric can be added to. An acidic modifier tends to lift, brighten and warm the colours, while an alkaline modifier can move colours toward green or pink, or mute or sadden them.

These generalisations are not applicable to all dyes, as some can react in quite unexpected ways with surprising results.

ACIDIC MODIFIERS

These tend to shift colours into warmer hues, towards yellow, orange or red. They include citric acid from lemon juice or clear/light vinegar, cranberry juice, tannic acid from oak galls, oxalic acid from rhubarb leaf, dock and sorrel (leaves, stems and roots), cream of tartar and tartaric acid.

ALKALINE MODIFIERS

These can move colours toward green or pink, or other unexpected shades, and can make colours more murky. They include wood ash, persimmon juice, baking soda, chalk (calcium carbonate), lime (calcium hydroxide), lye (sodium hydroxide) and soda ash (sodium carbonate). It can be interesting to use iron to modify colours to achieve black or dark hues that are otherwise difficult to achieve with dyes alone.

USING A MODIFIER

There are two basic methods for using a modifier.

Add modifier solution directly to the dye bath

1 Allow the dye bath to cool to room temperature. Mix in the required amount of modifier (usually 1–2 tsp or a jar-full, or see p42 for exact measures) directly into the dye bath. The dyed fibre should still be in the dye bath.
2 Gently move the fibre around, allowing the modifier to penetrate evenly all over. Open any folds and tease out any air bubbles which may cause the fibre to float above the surface.
3 Leave for several minutes to allow the colour to change. If a more dramatic colour change is required, leave to soak in the modifier for longer. Alternatively, repeat the above steps, adding more of the modifier solution.
4 Remove the fibre, wash with pH–neutral soap, rinse, wring to remove excess liquid, and hang to air dry out of direct sunlight.

Add dyed fibre to a seperate modifier bath

1 Allow the dye bath and fibre to cool. Fill a separate bowl with cool/warm water. Mix in the required amount of modifier (usually 1–2 tsp or a jar-full, or see p42 for exact measures).
2 Remove the fibre from the dye bath, wring to remove excess dye solution and place in the modifier bath. Gently move the fibre around, allowing the modifier to penetrate evenly all over.Open any folds and tease out any air bubbles which may cause the fibre to float above the surface.
3 Leave for several minutes to allow the colour to change. If a more dramatic colour change is required, leave to soak in the modifier for longer. Alternatively, repeat the above steps, adding more of the modifier solution.
4 Remove the fibre, wash with pH–neutral soap, rinse, wring to remove excess liquid, and hang to air dry out of direct sunlight.

Applying heat

If you're using plant fibres, you can apply heat to the modifier bath for 5–10 minutes to speed up the process. You can do the same for animal fibres and acidic modifiers. However, animal fibres are sensitive to alkaline modifiers, so it's best not to apply heat to avoid damage.

A piece of cloth showing true dye colour (dock) in the middle. The top has been dipped in alkaline modifier (soda ash), the bottom has been dipped in acidic modifier (vinegar)

Modifier recipes

ACIDIC MODIFIERS

See p40 for guidelines on how to use these modifiers.

Lemon juice or vinegar Use 1–2 tsp per 250g (9oz) of fibre.

Tannic acid from oak galls See recipe on p37. Use 1–2 tsp of the solution per 250g (9oz) of fibre.

Oxalic acid from rhubarb leaf/dock or sorrel leaf, root or stem See recipe on p34. Use 1–2 tsp of the solution per 250g (9oz).

Cream of tartar Dilute ½ tsp in just enough water to dissolve, and make a solution. Then use 1–2 tsp of the solution per 250g (9oz) of fibre.

Tartaric acid Dilute ½ tsp in just enough water to dissolve, and make a solution. Then use 1–2 tsp of the solution per 250g (9oz) of fibre.

ALKALINE MODIFIERS

Wood ash solution

You can easily make your own wood ash solution for use as an alkaline modifier.

Wood ash from a wood burner, fire pit or fireplace
2 plastic buckets or containers
Cheesecloth (optional)

1 Remove the cold ashes, making sure they are only wood ash. Place in a plastic bucket and fill with cold water. Leave to soak for 1 week, or until the liquid yellows and thickens.

2 Pour off the top level of liquid only into a separate bucket, leaving the bottom layer of sediment behind, or pour all the liquid through a cheesecloth to strain it.

3 Mix half a cup or jam jar of wood ash solution into a bowl of clean water – make sure there is enough liquid for the fibre to move around. This will create an alkaline modifier. To use this, you can simply lift your dyed fibre directly out of its dye bath, wring to remove any excess liquid, and add to the wood ash solution.

4 Alternatively, leave your fibre in the dye bath and allow the bath to cool. Then mix half a cup or jar of wood ash solution directly into the dye bath – this should be enough for a large dye bath and 200–500g (7–18oz) of fibre.

5 In either case, soak the fibre for 5–30 minutes, or until the desired shade has been reached. Turn constantly to allow the modifier solution to reach all areas of the fibre.

6 Remove the fibre and rinse it. Wash it with a pH-neutral soap and rinse it again, then hang it out to air dry.

Iron (ferrous sulphate powder) solution

Iron can be used as an alkaline modifier after the dyeing process to create darker tones – or sometimes black – and also as a mordant to improve colourfastness. It can be bought online as a powder.

When working with iron, be sure to keep a separate set of equipment to avoid contamination of other natural dye processes and projects.

Be careful when handling iron powder – it's caustic so it's advisable to wear a dust mask, gloves and eye protectors.

Scales
Iron powder (ferrous sulphate)
Old cup or jar
Bowl, spoon and tongs

1 Weigh the dry dyed fibre and note the weight. Then place the fibre in a large pot of water and allow it to soak for at least one hour, or ideally 8–12 hours/overnight, so that the fibre is pre-wetted.

2 Calculate 2% of the weight of the dry fibre – this figure will be the quantity of iron powder you need.

3 Put the iron powder into an old cup or jar and add hot water. Stir until dissolved.

4 Fill a bowl with cool/lukewarm water, enough for the fibre to move around in. Add the cup of iron water solution and stir in.

5 While it is still damp from dyeing, place the fibre into the bowl and make sure it is fully submerged. Leave to soak for 5–30 minutes until a dark enough shade is reached, turning constantly.

6 Remove the fibre and rinse it. Wash it with a pH-neutral soap and rinse it again, then hang it out to air dry.

Homemade iron water

If you prefer to make your own source of iron, rather than using ferrous sulphate, you can use the following recipe.

Rusty nails, or other small rusty iron objects
Sealable jar, and similarly sized pot
Clear vinegar

1 Place the small rusty metal objects inside a sealable jar. Pour in 1 part water and 2 parts vinegar to cover the objects. Seal the lid closed so it is airtight.

2 Once a day, pour the vinegar water out of the jar and into the other pot, leaving the rusty objects in the first jar. Leave the top of the jar open so they are exposed to air.

3 The next day, pour the same vinegar back into the jar with the rusty objects.

4 Continue to do this for 1 or 2 weeks, until the liquid has turned a rusty orange colour.

5 When it's ready to use, add 1 part iron water solution to 1 part clean water in a large bowl. Make sure there is enough liquid for the dyed fibre to move around in.

6 Soak the fibre for 5–30 minutes until a dark enough shade has been reached. Turn constantly to allow the modifier solution to reach all areas of the fibre.

7 Remove the fibre and rinse it. Wash it with a pH-neutral soap and rinse it again, then hang it out to air dry.

EQUIPMENT

SEPARATE EQUIPMENT

Most of the equipment used in dyeing is fairly familiar and found in most homes. However, it's best to reserve a completely separate set of pots, spoons and other equipment for dyeing only. This is particularly important when working with iron – any equipment used with iron should also be kept separate from your other dyeing equipment as it can change dye colours.

NON-REACTIVE EQUIPMENT

It's vital that all the equipment you use for natural dye processes is non-reactive. Stainless steel, heatproof glass and ceramic are the most reliable options. Reactive materials such as copper, tin and iron will react with dyes and cause colour changes. Throughout the book, all equipment listed refers to non-reactive options only.

STEAMING EQUIPMENT

Steaming a dyed fibre helps to set the colour (for hapazome, bundle dyeing, block printing and screen printing). If you have access to a professional fabric steamer or bullet steamer in a textile design studio, use it. I use a textile bullet steamer, but a vegetable or oriental rice steamer may also work as long as you don't mix it up with your kitchen equipment. Alternatively, you can fashion a makeshift steamer out of a stainless steel pot, lid and pasta insert/sieve/colander or cookie cooling rack. If this isn't possible, you can use a regular steam iron with a press cloth to protect the fibre.

A basic natural dye studio will require

Natural dye powder, extract powder, wood chips or other fresh or dried dye plant material
Mordants
Modifiers
Dye pots – large pots and pans
Large and small mixing bowls
Long-handled spoons
Tablespoons/teaspoons
Measuring spoons
Heatproof measuring jug
Sharp knives
Tongs
Sieve/strainer
Funnel
Pestle and mortar
Blender/food processor/coffee grinder
Scales
Calculator
Heat source – hot plate/stove
Iron
Ironing surface/table
Sealable jars
Lidded plastic storage buckets
Buckets and large plastic tubs
Airtight/sealable plastic boxes and plastic bags
Labels
Pens/pencils/ruler
Cleaning sponges and towels
pH-neutral soap
Eco laundry detergent or washing-up liquid
Rubber/protective gloves
Dust mask
Protective tablecloths
Apron
Protective eyewear
Gardening gloves
Scissors/secateurs
Gathering basket/foraging apron

TYPES OF DYE

Not all dyes bond with fibres in the same way – some fix to fibres readily with good colourfast results, but most require a little help from a mordant.

So as well as choosing the right fibre for your project, you should consider the type of dye that could work for your project. In the Dye Colours chapter (see p65), I've listed the type of dye each dye material produces.

Adjective dyes

These dyes won't fix to fibres well without the help of a mordant. When used in conjunction with a mordant, they will bond with fibres much better to produce long-lasting results. Examples include bracken, cochineal and nettle.

Substantive dyes

These dyes have naturally occurring fixative properties, such as tannins, which work as a natural mordant, allowing the dye to fix to the fibre. You can use substantive dyes with a mordant to improve results, but it's not always necessary to do so. Examples include eucalyptus and various tree barks such as oak, apple and cherry.

Vat dyes

Unlike all other dyes, these dyes are not soluble in water. The most obvious example is indigo, which instead is soluble in an alkaline environment from which the oxygen has been removed. It requires a slightly more complex process to achieve its beautiful hues, which you can find out about on p110–117. You don't need a mordant with indigo, as the colour fixes to the fibres with colourfast results.

Fugitive dyes

These are not really dyes in the true sense. They are merely stains, which lose colour, change or fade with time. They come from fresh or dried plant material such as flowers, beetroot, turmeric or blackberries. You can't pair them with a mordant to fix to fibres, so just simply embrace their ephemeral quality.

MAKING A DYE BATH

The term 'dye bath' is used to describe the dye solution or liquid which has been made using dye material. It is the extracted dye colour suspended in water.

GENERAL DYE BATH-MAKING TIPS

Dye material quantities Animal fibres take up dye colour more readily than plant fibres, so use slightly more dye material when dyeing plant fibres.

If you are unsure how much fresh dye plant material to use for your quantity of fibre, a ratio of 1 part plant material to 1 part fibre is a good starting point.

Each dye bath will require slightly different quantities of dye material – some guidelines are listed in the Dye Colours chapter on p65. However, the depth and quality of colour from your dye material will vary depending on where and when it was grown, the weather, climate, type of soil, time of year it was harvested and so on. It's therefore hard to predict or replicate exact colours.

Dye bath-making methods If you're unsure about how to turn a dye plant material into a dye bath, remember that most material will release colour if simmered in water for 1 hour. If a cold extraction is preferred, cover the material with boiling water to activate the process, leave for a few moments, then top with enough water to allow your fibre to move freely. Then leave for several days or weeks, or until a good depth of colour has been achieved.

Adding water to the dye bath The quantity of water used to make a dye bath isn't exact – you simply need enough for the fibre to move around in. You won't reduce the amount of colour in the dye bath by adding water. The same amount of colour remains for the fibre to absorb.

As a guideline, you'll need about 4–5 litres (1 gallon) of water in the dye bath for 100g (3½oz) of fibre. You need enough for the fibre to move around freely so that the dye can reach all of it consistently and evenly. If after you've made the dye bath you realise you don't have enough water, simply top up.

Bought materials

Dry dye materials can easily be bought online as wood chips and shavings, dye powder, extract powder, root, bark, insects and petals. Dye powder is simply dye material ground into powder, whereas extract powder is made up of dye particles that have been isolated and extracted from the original dye material – it is much stronger than standard dye powder.

DYE POWDER OR EXTRACT POWDER

About 1 tsp of dye powder or extract powder is enough to dye about 100g (3½oz) of washed, scoured and dried animal or plant fibre. But this can vary as natural dyeing isn't an exact science – you'll get the hang of quantities with experience and by using the recipes in this book.

1 Add the powder to a small bowl then add a few drops of hot water to make a paste. Mix well and work out lumps. Then slowly add more water to the paste until you have a liquid.

2 Once you have a liquid solution and the powder is thoroughly blended in, transfer it to the pot you will be dyeing in. Then pour in a few cups of warm water. Stir well to mix and evenly disperse the dye in the water.

3 Add enough water to allow the fibre to move freely. This is your dye bath. Choose your dye bath method on p58–59.

WOOD CHIPS AND SHAVINGS

You'll need about half the weight of the washed, scoured and dried fibre in wood chips. So if you have 100g (3½oz) of fibre, you'll need 50g (1¾oz) of chips.

1 Pour boiling water to just cover the chips. Then top up with enough water to allow your fibre to move freely.

2 Simmer for 1–2 hours, then leave to soak overnight.

3 Strain and reserve the chips for another future use. This creates your dye bath. Next, you can choose your dye bath method on p58–59.

From top left: Madder powder and dried madder root; Madder powder being turned into a paste; Adding water to madder powder; Madder powder dye bath

Found materials

Making dyes from natural materials is so simple. Like brewing tea, it requires the material to be chopped into small pieces, before steeping it in water. You can extract colour from pretty much anything that grows around you. Some colours may be more enchanting than others, but each has its charm.

If you can't forage or grow fresh dye materials, you can also buy them dried. Fresh material will often yield brighter results.

LEAVES

Leaves that work well include nettle, bracken and oak tree.

You can also try waste food such as carrot tops and spinach. And also herbs such as mint.

Try to use leaves that have already fallen to the ground, but any fresh, dry or frozen leaves are all fine too.

Use a ratio of 1 part leaves to 1 part washed, scoured and dry animal fibre, or a ratio of 2 parts leaves to 1 part washed, scoured and dry plant fibre.

1 Chop the leaves into shreds – the smaller you can chop them the better, as this allows for a greater amount of surface area from which the colour can be extracted into the water.

2 Add them to your dye pot. Just cover with boiling water. Wait a few moments and then fill the dye pot with enough warm water to allow the fibre to move around freely.

3 Leave to soak for 1–3 days, or until the water has turned a deep shade. Alternatively, apply heat for around 30 minutes.

4 Strain the leaves and use the liquid as the dye bath.

FRESH FLOWERS

Flowers that work well include hollyhocks, marigold and rose.

Use a ratio of 1 part flowers to 1 part washed, scoured and dry animal fibre. And a ratio of 2 parts flowers to 1 part washed, scoured and dry plant fibre.

You can extract colour from flowers by freezing them – see p103 for the full method. Or use the flowers as part of a bundle dyeing process, see p94–101 for the full method. Alternatively:

1 Add the flowers to a bowl of warm water (enough to allow the fibre to move around freely) and leave to soak overnight.

2 The next day, simmer the flower mixture for 30 minutes. Then leave to cool.

3 Strain out the flowers and use the liquid as the dye bath.

ROOTS

Roots that work well include dandelion, dock and madder root. You can use these fresh or dried.

Use a ratio of 3 parts roots to 1 part washed, scoured and dry animal or plant fibre.

1 If using fresh roots, scrub well to remove any mud. Chop them up into tiny chunks, so that you have the maximum amount of surface area from which the dye can escape into the dye bath. Add to your dye pot.

2 Just cover with boiling water. Wait a few moments, then fill the dye pot with enough warm water to allow the fibre to move around freely.

3 Leave to soak for 1–3 weeks, or until the water has turned a deep shade. Alternatively, apply heat for 1–2 hours.

4 Strain the roots and use the liquid as the dye bath.

NUTS OR BARK

Nuts that work well include, acorns, chestnut hulls and walnut husks. The best barks include apple (or any fruit tree) or oak.

Use a ratio of 3 parts nuts or bark to 1 part washed, scoured and dry animal or plant fibre.

1 Chop the nuts or bark into small pieces; if not possible, leave whole. Add to the dye pot.

2 Just cover with boiling water, wait a few moments, then fill the dye pot with enough warm water to allow the fibre to move around freely.

3 Leave to soak for 1–3 weeks. When a good colour has been reached, simmer the nut/bark mixture for 1 hour. Alternatively, don't soak, simply apply heat for around 1–2 hours.

4 Strain the nuts/bark and use the liquid as the dye bath.

BERRIES

Berries that work well include blackberries, blueberries and elderberries.

Use a ratio of 1 part berries to 1 part washed, scoured and dry animal or plant fibre.

1 In a dye pot, crush the berries to a pulp with a spoon. Cover with enough warm water to allow the fibre to move freely.

2 Place the lid on the dye pot and simmer the berry mixture for 1 hour.

3 Strain the liquid, being careful not to squash/push any of the berry fibre through the sieve. Use the liquid as the dye bath.

FOOD WASTE

Certain food waste is covered in the methods above. You could also try leftover red wine, which is a ready-made dye. Use it as it is – simply add your fibre before using a hot or cold dyeing method, see p58–59.

For peel (such as squash, beet, pumpkin, carrot and aubergine peel), follow the avocado dye bath recipe on p75.

Tea leaves or coffee grounds

1 Use a 1 part dye material to 1 part fibre.

2 Just cover with boiling water, wait a few moments, then fill the dye pot with enough water for the fibre to move freely.

3 Leave to soak for 1–3 weeks. Alternatively, simmer for 30–60 minutes.

4 Strain and use the liquid as your dye bath.

Shredding eucalyptus leaves

Eucalyptus leaves being picked, and steeping in a dye pot

DYE BATH METHODS

Once you have made the dye bath, there are various ways in which to dye the fibre – primarily either a cold dye method, or hot dye method. Where possible I always encourage using a cold dyeing process as it doesn't require an energy source.

ANIMAL FIBRES These take up dye colours very well and quickly. They are sensitive to heat, so tend to work well with cold dyeing or very gentle heat. Silk is likely to lose its sheen with high temperatures, and wool likely to shrink – keep at or below a simmer, and do not allow to boil. If you are using a cold dyeing method with animal fibres, it's best to use a strong dye bath with a higher percentage of dye material than you might require for hot dyeing.

PLANT FIBRES These are a little more stubborn when it comes to taking up colour. But they are much more sturdy than animal fibres, so a hot dyeing method is a good option.

For more on animal and plant fibres, and the best way to prepare them for dyeing, see the Fibres, Mordants and Modifiers chapter on p23.

COLD DYEING METHOD

1 Add the pre-mordanted and pre-wetted fibre to the dye bath, with the liquid at a cool or room temperature.

2 Leave to soak for 1–3 weeks, checking on the colour progress each day, until you have achieved the desired depth of colour. Remember that colours appear lighter once washed and dried.

3 Reserve the dye bath for another use if there is still colour in it. You can keep dye in a lidded bucket or sealed glass jar for several weeks. If mould appears, simply skim it off before dyeing. Alternatively, you can freeze it in a plastic box.

4 Rinse the fibre in lukewarm water, wash it with a pH-neutral soap, then rinse it again. Hang it to air dry, away from direct sunlight.

If this process doesn't work well for you, you can return the washed fibre (damp) back into the dye bath and follow the hot dyeing method opposite.

HOT DYEING METHOD

1 Add the pre-mordanted and pre-wetted fibre to the dye bath. Slowly raise the temperature of the dye bath to a simmer.

2 Simmer for 1 hour, gently stirring to allow the dye to reach all parts of the fibre – open up any folded areas, or sections that may be touching other areas of the fibre or the sides or bottom of the pot. Tease out any air bubbles that may have become trapped in the fibre causing it to rise above the surface.

3 Leave the fibre to sit in the dye bath overnight, and allow it to cool and the colour to saturate. Remove the fibre, gently wring out any excess dye liquid.

4 Reserve the dye bath for another use if there is still colour in it. You can keep dye in a lidded bucket or sealed glass jar for several weeks. If mould appears, simply skim it off before dyeing. Alternatively, you can freeze it in a plastic box.

5 Rinse the fibre in lukewarm water, wash it with a pH-neutral soap, then rinse it again. Hang it to air dry, away from sunlight.

SOLAR DYEING

If you live somewhere hot, or during warmer seasons, you can try using a solar oven to make use of the natural heating rays of the sun. Use a glass jar with a lid – ideally a dark coloured one, which will absorb the sun's heat best, although a clear glass jar can be used.

1 Place the fibre in the jar and fill it with the dye liquid. Seal shut with the lid.

2 Place the jar on a window ledge or outside in direct sunlight. Leave it for several days or weeks, until the desired colour is achieved.

ALL-IN-ONE DYEING

This method combines fresh dye plant material (leaves, bark, berries and such like) with the fibre.

1 Place the dye plant material in a large pot and cover with boiling water. Leave to soak for 1 hour. Fill with more warm water, so there is enough for the fibre to move freely.

2 After the material has soaked, leave it in the water (do not strain). Then follow the cold or hot dyeing method opposite.

3 Gently stir the pot regularly to keep the dye material from sticking to certain areas of fibre and creating patches of deeper colour. Alternatively, you can make use of this as a special pattern effect, and do less stirring!

LAYER DYEING/BUILDING COLOUR

If you've dyed the fibre and wish to have a deeper colour, follow these steps:

1 Allow the dye bath to cool, then remove the dyed fibre from the bath. Wash the dyed fibre with pH-neutral soap, then rinse with lukewarm/cool water.

2 Add another 1 tsp of dye or extract powder to the bath and stir to mix. If you're using additional dye plant material, steep it again, then strain out additional material. Then return the still-damp fibre to the dye bath to repeat the dye process.

Most fibres dye better with this multi-stage dye process, so it's good practice to layer-dye like this and build the colour up until you reach the desired shade, rather than to over-saturate the first dye bath with dye material.

For darker shades of colour, you can mordant the fibre for a second time after it's been dyed. Then layer-dye as above.

1 Wash the dyed fibre with pH-neutral soap, then rinse with lukewarm/cool water.

2 While the fibre is still damp, follow the relevant mordanting steps (p32). If the dyed fibre is dry, pre-wet (p30) before following the mordanting steps.

3 Return the damp fibre to the dye bath and repeat the dye process.

Madder powder dye bath with silk

Submerging silk in a madder dye bath using the cold dyeing method

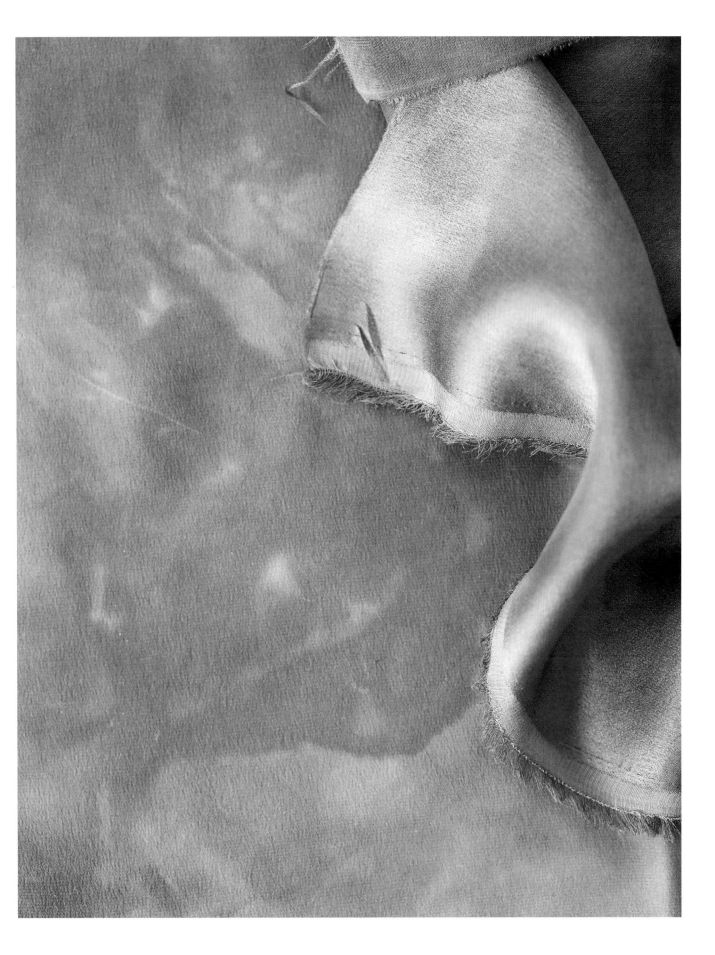

YARN AND PAPER

YARN DYEING

If you are dyeing yarn and it is not already in a skein, you will need to wind it into one so it will soak up the dye well with a consistent colour all over. You can use equipment such as a windmill-style skein winder, a niddy-noddy, a tabletop winder or umbrella swift, if you have access to any of these. Otherwise use of the back of a chair or your forearm to wind the yarn around. Make sure that whatever you use it is thoroughly clean before you start, and wind loosely, so that it is easy to remove the skein afterwards. Once you have wound off the skein, tie it loosely in four places, using a figure-of-eight fastening, which allows the yarn to move freely within the tie. You can then remove the skein from the winder. Doing all this properly will prevent the yarn from twisting and knotting in the pot, so it is well worth the effort.

1 Wash and scour the yarn (p30), but be careful not to go over a simmer to avoid shrinking the fibre.

2 Prepare the yarn with a mordant. You can use a plant-based mordant for strong and earthy colours, or a mineral-based mordant for brighter tones. See p32–38 for instructions. Yarn has a tendency to float, so it's important to make sure that all areas of it are submerged equally and receiving the mordant. You may find this easier to do by weighing it down with a small and non-reactive lid or plate. This also applies when it's in the dye bath.

3 Pre-wet the yarn by placing it in a large pot of water and allow it to soak for at least 1 hour, or ideally 8–12 hours/overnight.

4 Place the pre-wetted yarn into the dye bath. The dye pot should be large enough to let the yarn sit in without being squashed, and there should be enough liquid to cover it. You can add more water, if needed.

5 Apply gentle heat, remembering not to go above a simmer with delicate animal fibres, and don't shock the fibres by going from one extreme temperature to another.

6 With animal fibre yarns such as wool, it's important to avoid agitating the yarn too much, as this can result in felting and fluffing. Simply let the yarn sit in the dye bath for 30 minutes and then turn it over and let it sit for another 30 minutes.

7 If you wish to have a longer dye time than one hour, allow half the desired time for each side. This should also help to achieve an all-over coverage, as some yarns, especially woollens, tend to float to the surface of the dye pot.

8 Once you have achieved the desired depth of colour, turn off the heat. Leave the yarn in the dye pot to cool and saturate overnight.

9 After removing the yarn from the dye pot, it can be gently rinsed and washed with a pH-neutral soap and lukewarm water. Gently wring out any excess water and hang out the skein to air dry.

PAPER DYEING

1 Create a dye bath in a non-reactive shallow tray or dish – ceramic or glass is fine. It should be big enough to allow the paper to lie flat.

2 Lay the sheet of paper into the tray and tease it under the surface of the dye bath for a few seconds to absorb the colour. Don't leave the paper submerged in the liquid for a long period of time, as this could cause it to deteriorate and fall apart.

3 If you don't have a shallow tray, you can also use a large dye pot and lower the sheet into it vertically, again taking it out after a few seconds.

4 Air dry the paper by hanging it on a line with a couple of clips or pegs.

5 You can layer the dye by repeating the dye process after the first layer of colour has dried. This will allow the colour to deepen, without compromising the integrity of the paper.

6 Alternatively, you can apply dye colour to paper by brushing it on with a wide, flat brush. Apply a layer of colour, hang it to air dry, and then apply further layers of colour to achieve deeper shades.

Undyed yarn (left); yarn dyed with onion skin (right)

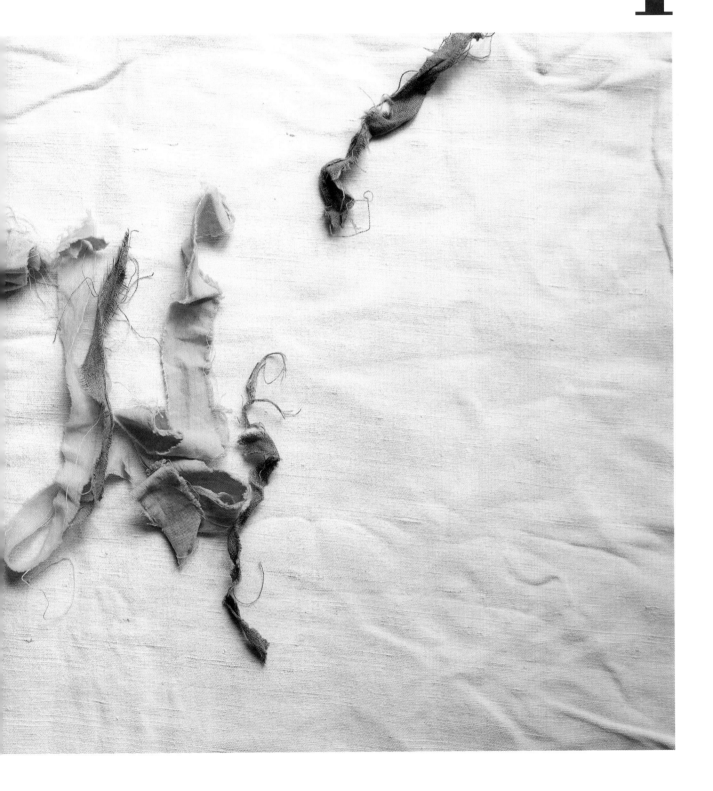

Fibre	Mordanted fibre	Sappanwood	Cochineal	Madder	Avocado	Red Dock

Wool with rhubarb leaf mordant

Silk with rhubarb leaf mordant

Wool with alum + cream of tartar mordant

Silk with alum + cream of tartar mordant

Cotton with oak gall mordant

Linen with oak gall mordant

Cotton with oak gall, alum + soda ash mordant

Linen with oak gall, alum + soda ash mordant

SAPPANWOOD

Sappanwood (*Caesalpinia sappan*), also known as Indian redwood, is a small, thorny, flowering tree from the Fabaceae legume family, which is native to Asia.

It's used in folk medicine (often as a pink drink made with ginger, cinnamon and cloves), and it's long been used for its antimicrobial and anti-allergenic properties: it's believed to protect against skin and joint infections, and food poisoning.

COLOUR The heartwood of the tree produces beautiful shades of pink and peachy pink through to bright reds and purply reds. It is much lighter in hue than its relation brazilwood (Paubrasilia), which you should avoid using as it is an endangered species.

SOURCE Source sappanwood dye from responsibly managed plantations in Asia. Sappanwood is generally available as a dye powder, an extract powder or as wood chips.

TYPE OF DYE/MORDANT Adjective dye.

Use the mordant that best suits the fibre you're dyeing.

Sappanwood has poor light-fastness, so avoid using on a dye project that will be exposed to sunlight, such as clothes. Its wash- and rub-fastness is good, and the colour holds well.

MAKING A DYE BATH

Extract powder
Weigh the fibre after it has been washed, scoured and dried. For a red, use 20% of the weight of the fibre in extract powder – for example, for 400g (14oz) of fibre, use 80g (3oz) of extract powder. For deep reds, use 50–100% of the weight of the fibre in extract powder.

See p53 for how to make an extract powder dye bath.

Wood chips
Weigh the fibre after it has been washed, scoured and dried. For a red, use 25% of the weight of the fibre in chips – for example, with 400g (14oz) fibre, use 100g (3½oz) chips. For a light red, use 10% of the weight of the fibre.

Add the chips to the dye pot and add enough boiling water to allow the fibre to move freely. Leave to soak overnight.

The next day, add a little more water to the pot and boil for 2–3 hours. Leave to sit again overnight before using.

Strain through a piece of muslin and use the liquid as the dye bath. Save the chips for soaking another time.

Dye powder
Weigh the fibre after it has been washed, scoured and dried. Use the same quantities of powder as wood chips (see above).

Add to a small bowl. Add a little water to turn the powder into a paste. Add a little more water to create a solution. Then transfer to a dye pot. Fill the pot with enough boiling water to allow the fibre to move freely. Leave to soak overnight.

The next day, add a little more water to the pot and boil for 2–3 hours. Leave to sit again overnight before using as a dye bath.

DYE BATH METHOD Suitable with a hot dyeing method. See p58–59 and follow the additional guidelines below.

For a dye bath made with extract powder, simmer the fibre in the dye bath for 60 minutes, stirring gently from time to time. Leave overnight to cool.

For a dye bath made with powder or chips, bring the dye bath to a simmer for 30-60 minutes.

If the dye results are orangey, you can add chalk powder (calcium carbonate) to the dye bath for a better pink/red. Add 1 tsp per 100g (3½oz) of fibre.

You can use the dye bath a second time to dye another fibre a peachy pink, or a third time for a pale pink.

MODIFIER Sappanwood is very pH-sensitive. It will react to acids by turning orange, and to alkalines by turning purple.

COCHINEAL

Cochineal (*Dactylopius coccus*) is a scale insect, indigenous to South and Central America, but also introduced to Spain, North Africa and Australia. It is thought to have been harvested by Aztecs and Mayans, and was once considered more precious than gold. A range of paintings and textiles found preserved in various ancient Mayan and Aztec pyramid tombs feature cochineal, while Aztec women would stain their teeth with the crushed bodies of the insects to appear more attractive.

The insects live on and feed off the nopal cacti, also known as the prickly pear, and they contain high levels of carminic acid as a natural defence against potential predators, which do not like the acidic taste. It's the female insect and eggs that are used to produce the colour, as they have much higher levels of carminic acid than the males – up to 17–24% of their body mass. The insects are collected individually by hand and then dried and crushed.

COLOUR Cochineal offers intense hues of scarlet, orange reds and bright pink. Depending on the method for drying the insect, a number of different colours can be achieved, which is why the shades of red vary so much across commercial suppliers. Cochineal can also be used to overdye indigo to get wonderful colourfast purples, or over madder to get a stronger red.

SOURCE Cochineal can be bought online either as whole dried insects, or as a dye powder or extract powder, and tends to be imported from Peru.

TYPE OF DYE/MORDANT Adjective dye.

Use the mineral-based mordant alum and cream of tartar to bring out a crimson tone (see p35). Otherwise use the mordant that best suits the fibre you're dyeing.

MAKING A DYE BATH

Weigh the fibre after it has been washed, scoured and dried, then follow the correct quantities opposite.

Dye powder (or whole dried cochineal ground into powder)
For a deep red, use 20–50% of the weight of the fibre in dye powder – for example, for 400g (14oz) of fibre, use 80–200g (3oz–7oz) of dye powder. About 5% gives a rich pink; and around 1% gives a light pink.

Extract powder
For a deep red, use 4% of the weight of the fibre in extract powder – for example, for 400g (14oz) of fibre, use 16g (⅓oz) of extract powder.

See p53 for how to make a dye powder and extract powder dye bath, and follow steps 1 to 4.

Once you have made the dye bath, leave it overnight. The next day, add a little more water and bring to a simmer for 15–20 minutes, keeping it below a boil.

If you're using whole cochineal, you may need to strain through a fine sieve or muslin. Use the liquid as the dye bath.

DYE BATH METHOD Suitable with either the cold dyeing method or hot dyeing method. See p58–59 and follow the additional guidelines below.

Cochineal is best used with soft water – hard water has a higher level of impurities in it that the carmine bonds to, giving paler dye results. So if you live in a hard water area use rainwater or distilled water for dyeing.

For the cold dye, leave to sit overnight in the dye bath. For the hot dye, apply a low heat for about 40 minutes.

After taking the fibre out of the dye bath, allow to cure for a couple of days before washing.

After you've dyed the fibre, you can use the dye bath a second or third time to dye another fibre a lighter pink.

MODIFIER Cochineal is very pH-sensitive. An acidic modifier shifts colours to orange and red. An alkaline modifier will shift hues to plum and purple.

MADDER

Madder (*Rubia tinctorum*) is native to Asia and Europe. Its genus name Rubia comes from the Latin word *ruber*, meaning 'red'. Madder was used as a medicinal plant by ancient civilizations and throughout the Middle Ages, and is still farmed for Ayurveda and Chinese medicine – it's believed to help alleviate blood disorders, jaundice, inflammation, kidney stones and dysentery, and to stimulate menstruation.

Its use as a dye can be dated back as far as the Ancient Egyptians, who buried King Tutankhamun with a cloth dyed red, and in Ancient China it can be dated to the Zhou Dynasty, more than 2,000 years ago. During the 18th century, the famous British army 'redcoats' were achieved using madder dye baths. It was only in 1869 that madder fell out of popularity, after scientists managed to synthesise the two separate dyes in madder, alizarin and purpurin, and later discovered anthraquinone, which allowed for the synthesis of a red pigment from coal tar to replace madder dye.

The plant is a small, evergreen, perennial shrub, growing up to 1.2m (4ft) tall, with pale yellow flowers. It likes to grow in rich, deep, well-drained soil, does well in wasteland and hedgerows, and is ready to harvest after three years once the green top has died back in autumn. High-alkaline soil encourages more pigment production in the roots. There are a few kinds of madder that you may come across: common madder (*Rubia tinctorum*), wild madder (*Rubia peregrina*) and Indian madder (*Rubia cordifolia*). All can be used for natural dyeing purposes, though Indian madder is known for being less strong in colour so is considered inferior.

COLOUR Madder can be used to produce a range of different reds, from orangey red to scarlet and brick red. The colour outcome will depend largely on how it was grown and processed, the quality of the soil and the age of the root. It will also depend on how much of it you add the to dye bath, the type of water you have access to (hard or soft) and the level of heat applied to the dye bath.

SOURCE You can buy madder online as dried root, or dye powder. But it's very easy to grow and can be used fresh or dried. The red-brown roots that grow up to 1m (3ft) long are the part that's harvested for dyeing. If you use fresh roots, wash them and then put them aside to dry and cure for a couple of months before grinding them down into a powder. You'll need about 1kg (2.2lb) of fresh madder to yield about 150g (5¼oz) of dried madder.

TYPE OF DYE / MORDANT Adjective dye.

You can achieve an aubergine shade by using a mineral-based mordant on your fibre before dyeing, and an iron solution as an after-mordant (see p42–43). Add roughly 1 jar of the iron solution to a dye bath of around 4–5 litres (1 gallon). A mineral-based mordant alone will give good reds, or use only an iron mordant for brownish red. Otherwise use the mordant that best suits the fibre you're dyeing.

MAKING A DYE BATH

Dried root
Weigh the fibre after it has been washed, scoured and dried. For a deep red, use 50–100% of the weight of the fibre in dried root – for example, for 400g (3½oz) of fibre, use 200–400g (1¾–3½oz) of madder root. For pale red, use 20% of the weight of the fibre in root – for example, for 400g (14oz) of fibre, use 80g (3oz) of root.

Grind it in a pestle and mortar or coffee grinder. Put the ground root into a cheesecloth and tie with string, like a makeshift tea bag, and place it in the dye pot. Fill with enough water to allow the fibre to move freely. The cheesecloth stops any larger particles from escaping, which might create inconsistencies in the dye results.

Leave for 24 hours. Alternatively, apply heat and simmer for 1 hour. After this time, remove the madder and use the liquid as the dye bath.

Dye powder
Weigh the fibre after it has been washed, scoured and dried. Use the same ratios and quantities as the dried root, above.

See p53 for how to make the dye powder dye bath.

DYE BATH METHOD Madder is suitable with either the cold dyeing method, hot dyeing method or the all-in-one dyeing method. See p58–59 and follow the additional guidelines below.

If you live in a soft water area you might have trouble reaching a good red. If so, try adding chalk powder (calcium carbonate) to the dye bath, to bring out the redder tones – add 1 tsp per 100g (3½oz) of fibre. Alternatively, use slightly lower temperatures with the hot dyeing method.

For the hot dye, heat for about 30–60 minutes. However, it's important to keep the temperature of the water below a simmer for reds, if it goes above a simmer it can create browns. And don't allow the water to boil. For the cold dye, leave for 2 days for a good red, or 3–4 days for a deeper shade.

After you've dyed the fibre, you can use the dye bath a second or third time to dye another fibre a lighter shade. In fact, it's good to have lots of fibre on hand in order to make the most of the multiple shades a madder dye bath offers.

MODIFIER Use an acidic modifier to shift the colours toward yellow and orange. An alkaline modifier can give pinker or redder tones.

AVOCADO

The avocado (*Persea americana*) is a tree fruit, a large berry with a single large seed. In ancient Mayan culture it was a fruit of mystical magic and fertility, associated with healing, love and beauty. It was believed to have such a powerful influence on female fertility that young virgins were banned from leaving the family home during harvest season. Due to the lasting impact of these old stories, it's said there was a campaign to change the cultural attitude towards the fruits during the 19th century, to boost the avocado industry.

Avocados are full of beneficial vitamins, minerals and antioxidants, including vitamins C and E. There are many different kinds, all of which are native to the tropics. The tree most likely originated in Mexico, but is now grown in many tropical and Mediterranean climates around the world.

The two kinds that are commonly imported are the Hass avocado, which has a thick, dark purplish brown skin and an oval shape, and the Fuerte avocado, which has a thinner, smoother skin with a brighter green colour.

Recycling avocado skins and pits, rather than tossing them straight into the compost or bin, is a wonderful way to get a second life out of them – they can always be given to the compost for their remaining nutrients after you've used them as a dye material.

COLOUR The peel of the avocado offers a pale dusty blush, while the pit offers a slightly deeper pink tone.

SOURCE Avocados can be difficult to grow as they prefer tropical climates and take at least 3–4 years to bear fruit. But luckily they're readily available in supermarkets. The peel and pit of all kinds of avocado can be used for their colour-giving properties. Instead of discarding them, collect them slowly over time as you use the fruit. You'll need to dry them or store them in a bag in the freezer until you are ready to use them. Alternatively, keep them submerged in water in a lidded bucket until you have collected enough for your dye bath.

TYPE OF DYE / MORDANT Substantive dye.

Because of its natural tannin content, avocado doesn't need to be paired with a mordant, but using one can deepen colours and strengthen the colourfastness of the dye. Use the mordant that best suits the fibre you're dyeing.

MAKING A DYE BATH

Weigh the fibre after it has been washed, scoured and dried. For a deep pink, use 200% of the weight of the fibre in peel and/or pit – for example, for 400g (14oz) of fibre, use 800g (28oz) of avocado.

Wash the peel and/or whole pit (don't crush or cut the pit). Place them in a dye pot, cover with enough warm water to allow the fibre to move freely. Bring to the boil and boil for 30–60 minutes.

Strain with a fine sieve or muslin and use the liquid as the dye bath.

DYE BATH METHOD Suitable with either the cold dyeing method or hot dyeing method. See p58–59.

MODIFIER Acidic modifiers may cause a subtle shift to orangey tones, while an alkaline modifier can take the colour towards brown. An iron modifier can even shift hues to black.

DOCK

Dock is of the same genus (*Rumex*) as sorrel and the same family as rhubarb. There are many species of *Rumex*, and many that can be used for dyeing.

Dock was originally found in the northern hemisphere, although many species have now been introduced all over the world. Although regarded as a weed, dock is known for its ability to soothe stings. It is found in waste grounds, near hedgerows, or on cultivated acid or calcareous soils. It grows to about 1m (1yd) tall and has leathery leaves that can be red or green.

Interestingly, dock has the chemical ability to transmute metallic iron into biological iron. So if you want to use a natural iron mordant in your work, you could place iron objects in the soil next to dock roots.

COLOUR The time of harvest will impact the dye results. I've used September-harvested red dock to get reddish-brown colours. At other times (or using other species of dock) may yield shades of olive green, orange, brown or yellow.

SOURCE Dock is regarded as an invasive species, so you will be doing your local farmer or gardener a favour by offering to remove these plants! But always ask the landowner first.

It's best to use the root, and winter is the best time to harvest. To spot the plant after it has died back, look for its long, tall stalk of flowers or seeds, which tower above the plant. After rainfall the ground should be easier to dig into to remove the roots. Mature plants will give the strongest colours – you'll be surprised by how much colour comes out of a small amount of chopped dock root. You can also use the seeds for dyeing, or reserve them for bundle-dyeing projects.

TYPE OF DYE/MORDANT Substantive dye.

Dock does not need a mordant to fix its colour to animal fibres, but you will need one for plant fibres, otherwise the colour will be very pale. Dock naturally contains biological iron, which saddens the dye colour results, so for brighter colours use the mineral-based mordant alum and cream of tartar (see p35). Rich and deep colours can be achieved with a plant-based mordant, such as rhubarb leaf or oak gall.

MAKING A DYE BATH

Fresh dock root
Weigh the fibre after it has been washed, scoured and dried.

For a dark shade, use 300% of the weight of the fibre in dock root – for example, for 400g (14oz) of fibre, use 1.2kg (42oz) of dock root.

Scrub the roots well to remove any mud. Chop them up into tiny chunks, so that you have the maximum amount of surface area from which the dye can escape into the dye bath. Put the chunks in the dye pot and cover with enough warm water to allow the fabric to move freely.

Boil for at least 2 hours. When boiling the roots, a strong, earthy aroma is produced that can be unpleasant to some, so work in a well-ventilated area.

After boiling, leave to soak overnight. The next day, boil again for 1 hour. Leave to cool.

Strain through a fine sieve or muslin and use the liquid as the dye bath.

DYE BATH METHOD Suitable with either the cold dyeing method, hot dyeing method or all-in-one dyeing method. See p58–59.

MODIFIER Depending on the species of dock that you use, modifiers will extend the range of colours only very subtly. An alkaline modifier such as iron can take colours into much darker tones, ranging from dark brown to grey and black.

ONION

Onion (*Allium cepa*) is an allium, from the family Liliaceae. It is found on every continent and may have been growing wild everywhere since pre-civilisation. It's thought that the Ancient Egyptians believed the onion bestowed strength and that its concentric spherical rings symbolised eternity. In Alexandria, the royal army apparently ate onions to improve vitality, while the Romans gained strength and courage from these little golden orbs. There are a range of old folk recipes that praise onion juice droplets as a cure for earache, a piece of raw onion on the forehead to reduce migraine, and onion in a compress wrapped in cheesecloth on the chest to remove coughs. It's said that in some rural places, onions were strung up in houses as protective magical amulets against sickness.

Brown and red onions are a classic home-dyer's choice – there's always a plentiful supply, and the colour they give is surprisingly rich – making them a favourite when you want an impressive result with little effort.

COLOUR Brown skins make beautiful yellow tones when kept below a boil, while boiling the skins can provide rich burnt orange and rust-coloured dyes (this is what I've used for the fabrics in the image, left). Red skins offer slightly plummier tones. When used together, they create a vibrant, multi-dimensional hue.

SOURCE Onions are easy to grow from sets and take about three to four months to be ready to harvest. You can use the skins for colour. Store up supplies of onion skins from your own cooking – or if you need more, ask a local greengrocer for the waste from the bottom of their boxes, or go to cafés or food producers and ask them to put aside a bag for you. Apparently, over 500,000 tonnes of onion waste is thrown away every year in Europe. Imagine how much dye we could be making with all of that?

Store dry onion skins in paper bags, cardboard boxes or similar. Just make sure that it's only the dry skins you have, and not any of the fleshy bits, and that they are fully dried out before going into storage, or things can get really smelly.

TYPE OF DYE/MORDANT Substantive dye.

Onion doesn't need to be paired with a mordant, but using one can deepen colours and strengthen the colourfastness of the dye. You should use the mordant that best suits the fibre you're dyeing.

MAKING A DYE BATH

Weigh the fibre after it has been washed, scoured and dried. For a deep shade, use 50% of the weight of the fibre in skin – for example, for 400g (14oz) of fibre, use 200g (7oz) of onion.

Onion skins are super-easy and quick to dye with. No need to chop them, simply put them in the dye pot and pour in enough water to allow the fibre to move freely.

Bring to a simmer, and simmer for 30 minutes. You'll see the colour of the water changing and deepening quite quickly.

Strain out the onion skins and use the liquid as the dye bath.

DYE BATH METHOD Suitable with the hot dyeing method. See p58–59 and follow the additional guidelines below.

For the hot dye, simmer for about 30 minutes, or until you have the desired shade.

You can use the dye bath a second time to get paler shades.

MODIFIER An acidic modifier will shift colours towards orangey yellow. An alkaline modifier will move colours towards green.

EUCALYPTUS

Eucalyptus is named for its cup-like buds, after the Greek word *eucalyptos*, meaning 'well covered'. Australian Aboriginal people have used eucalyptus from time immemorial to treat fevers and all kinds of ailments. The essential oil is generally distilled from the leaves and has medicinal and antibacterial properties. It is one of the oils most commonly used in aromatherapy, and it's often used by herbalists to help loosen congestion and ease coughs: it's inhaled over steam baths, or used topically to relieve muscle and joint pains.

For more spiritual uses, eucalyptus makes a lovely smudge stick for purifying spaces in preparation for sacred rituals and ceremonies. Alternatively, it's great for clearing the air after an argument!

You could try hanging an unused branch of eucalyptus over your shower, for a refreshing bathing ritual experience. I love having it around to decorate gifts, hang on the wall or put into flower arrangements and bouquets, offering interactive olfactory sensations to passers-by.

There are over 400 species, but *Eucalyptus globulus* is the most commonly found – it is often introduced to new places, as it does so well in poor soil conditions. It also grows rapidly – it can be harvested in 14–16 years (compared to the usual 60 years of other trees), making it an appealing option for renewable timber. If you want to plant your own, it is worth considering that it is an invasive species and can damage plant diversity.

COLOUR Eucalyptus dye colours range from deep orange to reddish-brown from the leaves, and lighter hues of pinky-beige from the bark. I've used leaves to dye the fabrics in the image on the right.

SOURCE You can harvest the leaves at any time of the year, and they are best collected from the ground after they have fallen from the branches. They can be used even after the leaf colour has faded to brown, as the dye pigment is still in the leaf.

TYPE OF DYE/MORDANT Substantive dye.

The rich tannin content of the plant gives substantive qualities, meaning that mordants aren't essential, but they can be used to extend the life of colours and to obtain a wider range of shades. Use the mordant that best suits the fibre you're dyeing.

MAKING A DYE BATH

Weigh the fibre after it has been washed, scoured and dried. For a good deep shade, use 100% of the weight of the fibre in leaves or bark – for example, for 400g (14oz) of fibre, use 400g (14oz) of eucalyptus. For a dye bath using bark, follow the instructions on p54–55.

For a dye bath using leaves, chop the leaves up very small so they look shredded – the smaller you can chop them the better, as this allows for a greater amount of surface area from which the colour can easily be extracted into the water.

Place the finely chopped leaves into a dye pot and just cover with boiling water. Wait a few moments before topping up with enough warm water to allow your fibre to move freely. Simmer for 2–3 hours. Then leave to sit overnight. Strain through a fine sieve or muslin and use the liquid as a dye bath.

DYE BATH METHOD Suitable with the hot dyeing method or the all-in-one method. See p58–59 and follow the additional guidelines below.

For hot dyeing, bring to a boil for 2–3 hours (keep at a simmer for an animal fibre), before leaving overnight.

The discarded leaves can be used again to create a second dye bath.

MODIFIER An acidic modifier will give pinky shades, while an alkaline modifier will move colours toward muddier browns.

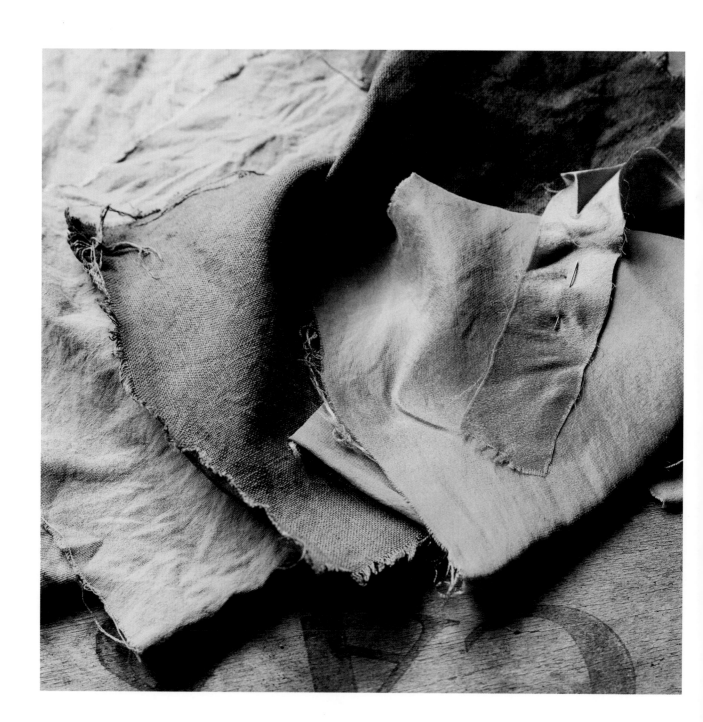

BRACKEN

Bracken (*Pteridium aquilinum*) is a type of deciduous fern – it's one of the oldest ferns known, with fossils recorded that date back over 55 million years. It was once believed to bring eternal youth and invisibility to the possessor, as mentioned in Shakespeare's *Henry IV*: 'We have the receipt of Fern seed – we walk invisible.'

In many Asian cultures the young shoots, known as 'fiddleheads', are eaten – for example, in Korea they are mixed into the traditional dish bibimbap. Others use the root, which can be ground down to give a starchy flour for making bread or jellies. Ancient civilisations used both the fronds and stems in medicinal drinks, and they are still used in a traditional wild beer in various countries, including Russia and Norway.

Do note, however, that there are noxious compounds in both fronds and roots, and they should not be eaten. The spores on the underside of the leaf are considered carcinogenic if regularly breathed in, but do not pose high risks if you're casually visiting an area planted with bracken.

Easily recognised by its large triangular fronds, which often grow up to 2m (8ft) high, bracken is commonly found on moorland across most continents. It's seen by some as an invasive plant, as it colonises land quickly driving out other species of moorland plant, while others appreciate the canopy it offers to other plant life where woodland no longer exists. For those with access to bracken-laden land, it's worth knowing its high potash content means it can be used as a valuable green manure.

COLOUR Bracken gives a range of yellow-green to olive green and greeny-brown shades. The colours will vary from place to place and depending on the time of year you harvest – I've had a random mixture of browns, yellow-browns, olive greens and coppery-greens from different batches.

SOURCE Bracken fronds can be harvested throughout the growing season, before they die back in the autumn/winter. Avoid harvesting in late summer when spores are released.

Bracken fronds are tough and can be sharp against the skin, so always wear gloves when harvesting them, and use a pair of scissors or secateurs to chop them at the nodules where the leaves join the stem.

Always ask the landowner before harvesting, and look out for local farmers who may be cutting back the bracken at certain times of the year – a great opportunity to recycle unwanted plant material.

TYPE OF DYE / MORDANT Adjective dye.

It's best to use a mordant with bracken to get deeper hues and longer-lasting results. Use the mordant that best suits the fibre you're dyeing.

MAKING A DYE BATH

Weigh the fibre after it has been washed, scoured and dried. For a deep shade, use 100% of the weight of the fibre in fresh, feathery fronds – for example, for 400g (14oz) of fibre, use 400g (14oz) of bracken.

See p54 for how to make a dye bath using leaves.

DYE BATH METHOD Suitable with the hot dyeing method. See p58–59.

MODIFIER An acidic modifier will produce lighter shades, while an alkaline modifier gives rich and deep red brick tones.

Nettle (*Urtica dioica*) is a much undervalued wild perennial with numerous useful qualities, from providing a tough fibre for rope, to its high nutritional value.

It's thought nettles were once used to mark the dwelling places of fairies and other magical creatures. Their protective energy could be used to dispel dark magic – or deter naughty spirits from causing mischief – by sprinkling the leaves about one's home or carrying the dried leaf on the body in a pouch.

Herbalists have traditionally used nettles to tackle hayfever, heart conditions, high blood pressure, arthritis, kidney and bladder problems and slow circulation, as well as to help balance blood sugar and cortisol levels.

Nettles are much higher in iron and vitamin C than many of the other more obvious sources, so they're a great addition to your diet to help increase mineral uptake. I like to gather extra nettles to make into a soup or pesto, especially at the beginning of the growing season. You can try collecting and drying them, and keeping a pot of the dried seeds to sprinkle on your food for added minerals and vitamins.

COLOUR The colours that nettles offer will vary from hues of yellowish green if harvested in early spring, to olive green if harvested in the late summer (the colour often becomes darker in tone later in the year). The soil they grow in, the weather and the climate all play a role in the outcome of the colours. You can also use the root to make a bright yellow dye.

SOURCE When harvesting the plant use gloves to protect your hands from being stung. Use normal household scissors to snip off the first two tiers of leaves, or the top six inches of the plant – I aim for the nodes as the place to cut, which is where the leaves join the stem. If you cut the stem at this point, you will encourage a new growth of leaves.

I use a basket to collect the leaves, then give it a bit of a shake and leave it on the ground for an hour before processing so that any tiny stowaway bugs and insects have a chance to escape!

TYPE OF DYE / MORDANT Adjective dye.

Use the mordant that best suits the fibre you're dyeing.

MAKING A DYE BATH

Weigh the fibre after it has been washed, scoured and dried. You'll need 200% of the weight of the fibre in fresh leaves – for example, for 400g (14oz) of fibre, use 800g (24oz) of nettle.

See p54 for how to make a dye bath using leaves.

Once you have made and strained the dye, you can use any leftover plant material as a green manure or compost to enrich the soil in your garden. Or make a liquid feed for garden plants by simply soaking it in water for 1–3 weeks then straining it to get a fertiliser liquid.

DYE BATH METHOD Suitable with the hot dyeing method. See p58–59.

MODIFIER Use iron as an alkaline modifier to get a deep, earthy green, or try an acidic modifier for warmer colours.

NETTLE

CHLOROPHYLLIN

The name chlorophyllin comes from the ancient Greek chloros meaning 'green', and phyllon, which means 'leaf'. Chlorophyll is responsible for the alchemical process of photosynthesis, in which light from the sun is converted within the plant cells into biological energy.

Chlorophyllin is a green pigment, which is extracted from plants such as nettle, alfalfa and mint, and has long been used as an alternative topical medicine for wounds and burns, in natural beauty products as a deodorant and for skin protection.

It's relatively new as a dye for textiles and crafts, but has been readily adopted by the natural home-dyeing community, as green has historically been the hardest colour to achieve. Previously, dyers would overdye indigo (blue) with weld (yellow), which would result in an earthy green, rather than the vivid and vibrant shade of chlorophyllin.

COLOUR Chlorophyllin produces a range of greens, from pale tones to deep forest and emerald sea.

SOURCE You can buy chlorophyllin online as extract powder.

TYPE OF DYE / MORDANT Adjective dye.

Use with a mordant to lengthen the life of the colours. Use the mordant that best suits the fibre you're dyeing.

MAKING A DYE BATH

Weigh the fibre after it has been washed, scoured and dried. For a good green, use 5% of the weight of the fibre in extract powder – for example, for 400g (14oz) of fibre, use 20g (½oz) of chlorophyllin.

See p53 for how to make an extract powder dye bath.

DYE PROCESS Suitable with the hot dyeing method. See p58–59 and follow the additional guidelines below.

For deeper colours, it's best to layer the colour (see p59).

Simply mordant the fibre again after dyeing and return to the dye bath. This is better than adding more extract powder to the first dye bath.

MODIFIER Chlorophyllin is very pH-stable and therefore doesn't change colour dramatically when acidic or alkaline modifiers are applied.

WELD

Weld (*Reseda luteola*) is a native plant of Europe and Asia, but has been naturalised around the world. The name *reseda* means a healer or restorer – it literally translates to 'gives comfort' in Latin. The Romans used it medicinally for its narcotic value, as a sedative and poultice, and to treat bites, stings and small wounds.

Its yellow dye is one of the oldest known in the world, along with madder and indigo – it was used by the Ancient Greeks and the Romans, who are believed to have dyed the robes of their Vestal Virgins with it. Its use as an ink can be traced back to medieval manuscripts, in which it was used for illumination, and by Vermeer in his painting Girl with a Pearl Earring.

The rich levels of luteolin are what give weld its bright yellow dye colour. This was eventually synthesised by scientists at the end of the 20th century, although weld had already fallen out of popular use following the invention of coal tar-derived dyes in the late 19th to early 20th century.

The plant is a yellow-flowering biennial, growing up to 1.5m (5ft) tall. The flowers give off an incredible sweet aphrodisiac scent, and are loved by bees, butterflies and insects. They are dried for use in potpourri and the fragrant oil is used in perfume, as well as an oil for lighting.

COLOUR Weld gives a brilliant bright yellow, which is often used for overdyeing indigo-dyed fibres to create beautiful emerald, leaf green and teal – and famously to create the Lincoln Green of Robin Hood's clothing, and another medieval hue, Saxon Green. It can also be used to overdye madder-dyed fibre to create oranges.

The quality of the local water you are using will dictate the outcome of the dye colour to some extent, as will the type of soil the plant has grown in.

It is soluble in hot water and alcohol, so it's great for use as a drawing ink as well as a dye (see p148).

SOURCE All parts of the plant are used, especially the tops, which flower in June to August. However, most of the dye is found within the seed, which is harvested as the flowers start to disappear at the end of the summer.

The best colour comes from plants with yellow or greenish flowers and an abundance of foliage. When handling the plant wear gloves, to avoid potential irritation to sensitive skin. Weld can be used either fresh or in dry form. You can source dried weld online.

TYPE OF DYE/MORDANT Adjective dye.

Yellow tends to be the dye colour that fades most quickly, but weld has proved to have better colour fastness than other sources of yellow. It's still best used with a mordant to lengthen the life of the colour. Use the mordant that best suits the fibre you're dyeing.

MAKING A DYE BATH

Dried
Weigh the fibre after it has been washed, scoured and dried. Use 50% of the weight of the fibre in dried weld – for example, for 400g (14oz) of fibre, use 200g (7oz) of weld.

Break up the weld and leave it to soak overnight in warm water.

The next day, chop up the weld and cover with enough water to allow the fibre to move freely. Bring it up to a simmer, and then simmer for 1 hour. Be careful to not let the liquid boil, as this will mute the weld colour from bright to murky.

Stir gently every now and then to encourage extraction from all parts of the plant material. After this, strain through a fine sieve or muslin and use the liquid as the dye bath.

Fresh
Weigh the fibre after it has been washed, scoured and dried. You'll need 50% of the weight of the fibre in fresh weld – for example, for 400g (14oz) of fibre, use 200g (7oz) of weld.

Chop the leaves, flowers and stalks and add to the dye pot with enough water to allow the fibre to move freely.

Bring it to a simmer, put the lid on the pot, and then simmer for 30 minutes. Be careful to not let the liquid boil, as this will mute the colour from bright to murky.

Strain and use the liquid as the dye bath.

DYE BATH METHOD Suitable with the hot dyeing method. See p58–59 and follow the additional guidelines below.

Simmering for 30–60 minutes will give yellow, but boiling for the same time will give a mustard hue.

If you find it difficult to achieve a bright, light yellow, try adding a small amount of chalk powder (calcium carbonate) to the dye bath. Keep the fibre in the dye bath, add about 1 tsp per 100g (3½oz) of fibre. Stir, then simmer for 1 hour more.

You may also find that a slightly longer dyeing time improves the colour.

As weld is slightly soluble in hot water, dyed items should always be washed in cold water only.

MODIFIER Both acidic and alkaline modifiers give clearer and brighter yellows. An iron solution used as a modifier will move the colour toward a moss or murky green.

LOGWOOD

Logwood (*Haematoxylum campechianum*) is native to Mexico and Central America, especially the Gulf of Campeche, but in 1715 it was introduced to Jamaica and various other Caribbean islands and naturalised.

Visually, you can identify this small flowering tree by its crooked, spiny branches, dark and roughly textured bark, small yellow flowers and the interesting leaf formation of heart-shaped pairs.

The part used by dyers is the inner heartwood of the tree, which is a rich red colour – hence its name from the Greek haima, meaning blood, and xylon meaning wood. The heartwood was exported to Europe from the 17th to the 19th centuries for use as a dye material, although now it's less valuable to commercial exporters. However, it is still widely used for its haematoxylin, which is used by scientists for the staining of plant and animal cells for observation.

COLOUR Logwood offers lovely soft shades of violet, deeper purples and bluey-black. Shades of purple will vary a lot, depending on the type of fibre, water and mordant, and purple can only be achieved when heat is applied, otherwise it yeilds black.

SOURCE Many logwood exports are sourced from an unsustainable logging industry, so if you choose to work with logwood it's important that you source the material from certified organic, fairtrade and sustainable sources.

You can use either logwood extract powder, or the wood chips, both available online.

TYPE OF DYE / MORDANT Substantive dye.

It's best to use a mordant with this dye, as it's not very colourfast. An iron solution used as a mordant is more helpful for extending the life of the colour and for achieving darker shades of blue and black.

MAKING A DYE BATH

Logwood extract powder is potent and you'll only need a very minimal amount to dye with.

Weigh the fibre after it has been washed, scoured and dried. You'll need 2% of the weight of the fibre in extract powder – for example, for 400g (14oz) of fibre, use 8g (⅙oz) of logwood. Or for dried chips, use 30% of the weight of the fibre.

You can use less for paler tones, but if you want a darker colour, it's best to layer dye the fibre to build up the colour (see p59).

See p53 for how to make a extract powder or wood chip dye bath.

DYE BATH METHOD Suitable with the hot dyeing method. See p58–59 and follow the additional guidelines below.

Bring the dye bath to a simmer for 45 minutes to 1 hour, then leave it to soak overnight.

You can dry any left-over plant material to keep for future use.

Do note that logwood is particularly pH-sensitive, so it's worth considering its suitability for different projects. It may not be the best option for clothing, as small splashes of salad dressing can change your look quite quickly!

MODIFIER Because logwood is so pH-sensitive, it will turn from light purple to brown with an acidic modifier, and move toward a deep purple with an alkaline modifier. Iron gives good bluey-blacks.

BUNDLE DYEING

Bundle dyeing, also known as eco-printing, is a contemporary process developed by Australian textile artist India Flint. As a child she would enjoy the traditions of her Latvian heritage, including dyeing Easter eggs with onion skins and imprinting them with leaves and herbs. As an adult, she applied the concept to fabric, and found that the plant dyes gave direct impressions, just as with the eggs.

This wonderfully alchemical process uses the botanical dyes from fresh flowers, leaves and other plant material to create herbal-infused prints. The print is formed when the plant transfers its colour onto the fabric (or paper). So the usual need for dye extraction or use of the dye bath is entirely skipped out, making this a particularly quick technique.

Mesmerising repeat patterns can be made with the use of different folding, rolling and binding styles, offering brilliantly unique prints. And because the results are so unpredictable, this is a great opportunity to be playful and experimental, and for using mindfulness and intuitive herbalism to guide you in your creative journey.

Many flowers will give bright, exciting hues to begin with, but they tend to fade after they have dried, are washed or age a little. You will find that some are more colourfast than others, and I invite you to go out and explore your local bio-region, to discover your own colour palette and learn which are your favourite plants to use for their colour, shape, fastness or herbal characteristics.

YOU WILL NEED
Fabric (washed, scoured and mordanted)
Clear or light-coloured vinegar in a mister bottle
Plant material (fresh petals, leaves, stems, berries and such like)
Dye powder or extract powder (optional)
Dried flowers (optional)
String or rubber bands
Steaming equipment (for hot dyeing)
Tongs
Glass jar with lid or plastic bag (for cold dyeing)

PLANT MATERIAL A wide variety of fresh and dried flowers and plants can be used for this technique. I like to use rich, dark-coloured flowers, especially viola, delphinium, iris, pelargonium, petunia, black-purple hollyhock, dark red roses, cornflower, marigold, passion flower, heather, chrysanthemum and geranium. You can use other plant parts too, such as berries, leaves, roots and seeds and even some waste foods such as onion skins.

I really enjoy building up seasonal layers of prints by foraging the things around me, through the different parts of the year, and creating a story of the different plants that have come and gone, leaving their impression behind on my cloth.

Most natural dye and extract powders work well when sprinkled lightly onto the surface too. Their intense colour tends to bleed and saturate well, so very little is required.

FABRIC Silk (animal fibre) is ideal for this technique. It absorbs the plant colour and holds on to it very well, too. I recommend you start out by using an organic, soft, tightly woven silk, such as a habotai, satin or crêpe de chine, although any kind of tightly woven animal fibre should work well. You can use plant fibres, too, such as hemp or linen, but they will need a longer mordanting and dyeing process.

MORDANT Silk doesn't necessarily need a mordant, however it's worth considering using one if you intend to use the fabric to make a garment that you'll wear a lot, or if the fabric will be exposed to lots of sunlight.

Using a mineral-based mordant such as alum and cream of tartar (see p35) will help brighten the colours and extend their life. I also like to use rhubarb leaf mordant as it gives the finished piece beautiful muted tones, which can be easier to wear if you're turning your printed fabric into a garment.

MODIFIER You could use a modifier such as iron water – this mutes the colours and gives the finished bundle-dye a melancholy, bluish tinge (see the bundle-dyed scarf on p174).

PROCESS

1 Make sure the fabric is washed and scoured, and mordanted. You can use it while it's still damp from the mordanting process. If the fabric is dry, pre-wet it (see p30) first, as this helps the colours to move through the fabric well.

2 Lay it out so that the whole piece of fabric is spread out before you on a table. If space is limited, you can work on one section of the fabric at a time.

3 Use a mister bottle to spray the fibre with vinegar until it is saturated. Vinegar has an acidic pH, which means that it helps to brighten colours. I use organic apple cider vinegar as it's local to me, though you can use any vinegar that's suitable for you. Just avoid the darker kinds, such as balsamic vinegar, as it isn't as effective at brightening the colours.

4 Scatter the plant materials across the cloth as you wish, perhaps breaking up petals and leaves or sometimes leaving them whole. I tend to be quite random about what I do, and get really into the process of enjoying making a mess with beautiful natural things! Some people like to make pretty arrangements and motifs with their leaves and flowers, but it never comes out quite as they might expect. It's always a surprise when you open the bundle later, and it's really impossible to control the exact outcome. The best thing is to experiment. Try out a few different techniques for scattering and arranging the plant material.

5 It's nice to leave a little blank space between the materials, instead of totally covering the surface; some space gives definition to the pattern. But do try to bring the plant material right up to the edges, so that you don't end up with an empty border around the sides. You can also sprinkle dye powder or extract powder onto the fabric.

6 Once you have scattered material across the piece, spray it again with vinegar. You can then start to bundle it up – there are a million ways you can try, but I like to use two different techniques for this.

Spraying the fabric with vinegar; Scattering plant material

Concertina fold

1 This method creates interesting symmetrical repeat patterns by folding the cloth like an accordion. To do this, concertina fold (as if you were making a fan with a sheet of paper) the piece of fabric back and forth until you have a narrow length of cloth.

2 Turn it vertically to face you, then concertina fold the narrow length of fabric until you have a small, square-ish bundle.

3 Alternatively, you can fold the fabric in half and in half again and again and again, until it can't be folded up any smaller. You can add more petals into each new fold if you wish, to create more layers of pattern, or you can leave it with just the initial layer. Give it a little spray with vinegar with each new fold.

4 Once you have made the bundle, use some string or rubber bands and secure it tightly. The idea is that you want the fibre and the plant material to be as closely pressed together as possible, so that the dye can transfer from one to the other.

Rolling

1 This method gives a more linear repeat pattern. Starting at one end of the fabric, roll it into a sausage shape with the plant material inside. Do this as tightly as possible.

2 Once you've rolled it one way, turn it vertically to face you, and then roll it again, as tight as you can, to make a spiral shape. You may like to do a bit of both: some folding and then a bit of rolling. There are no rules! Only endless ways to try.

3 Once you have made the bundle, use some string or rubber bands and secure it tightly. You want the fibre and the plant material to be as closely pressed together as possible.

COLD DYEING METHOD Simply put the bundle into a glass jar with a lid, or a plastic bag firmly tied closed, and leave for several weeks. At least one week, or until you can't bear to wait any longer! If mould starts to appear, this can be remedied by taking the bundle out of the jar or bag and putting it in the freezer, or steaming it for 30 minutes. Then put it back in the jar or bag and carry on with the process.

HOT DYEING METHOD Steaming the bundle speeds up the dye process. See p46 for steaming tips. Steam for one hour, turning it over every 15 minutes. Then turn off the heat and leave it to cool.

COMPOST DYEING METHOD I prefer to use a zero-energy approach for bundle dyeing. Wrap the fabric up in a protective cloth or bag. Dig a hole in a compost heap, then place the protected fabric in the hole and cover with more compost. The natural acids and heat mix with and morph the botanical colours into really interesting hues. Leave for a few weeks or months – simply come back to it when you remember, or when curiosity gets the better of you. If mould starts to appear, follow the remedy from the cold dyeing method, then return the bundle to the compost heap.

SOLAR DYEING METHOD Another great low-energy technique for applying heat. Place your bundle into a lidded, sealed glass jar. Leave on a window sill for several weeks, where it can catch the sun's warming rays.

POST-DYEING

1 Once you have completed the dye process, unwrap the bundle outdoors so you can shake off the plant materials.

2 Hang the fabric to air dry in a shady spot, out of direct sunlight. Once dry, remove any last pieces of plant material stuck to the fabric.

3 Use a steam iron and press cloth to steam press it.

4 I find that if I then hang the piece up somewhere dry, out of direct sunlight for a couple of weeks, the curing process really helps to extend the life of the colours. You may find that some colours are fugitive and change over time, while others are more reliable and last for years in the same state. In any case, the longer you leave the cloth to cure before washing it, the more longevity the colours will have.

5 After this curing, the fabric can be hand washed with some cool or lukewarm water and a gentle pH-neutral soap.

From top left: Concertina fold; Folding the fabric; Rolling method; The final rolled and concertina-folded bundles

Left, concertina fold; right, rolling

ICE FLOWER DYEING

Extracting colour from flowers can be difficult. You may find that applying heat to delicate petals disrupts their bright hues and causes a loss of colour. Using a cold extraction technique can be more successful, especially if you start by freezing the flowers – the drop in temperature causes a natural decomposition of the plant cells, making it easier for the colour to pass through into the dye bath.

This is not a very colourfast way to dye fabrics, but it's fun and easy to overdye fabric in order to create layers of colours. When the colour of a dyed fabric fades, you can overdye using this technique to give it a fresh burst of vibrancy.

It's also a good way to get a second life from used flowers from your home or garden, or waste flowers from the local florist. If they are wilting or slightly past their best, they are still fine to use for colour.

YOU WILL NEED

Plant material (fresh flowers and petals)
Netting bag or old tights (optional)
String
Freezer bag or airtight container
Pot or bowl
Fabric (washed, scoured, mordanted and pre-wetted)
Strainer
Press cloth
Steam iron
pH-neutral soap

PLANT MATERIAL Try deep-coloured flowers such as petunia and delphinium, or red rose and hollyhock.

FABRIC This technique works best on silk (animal fibre) as it absorbs colours easily and holds onto them well.

MORDANT For silk, use mineral-based mordant alum and cream of tartar (see p35), to brighten the colours.

PROCESS

1 Put the fresh flowers and petals inside a netting bag, or old tights tied with string – doing this is optional, but it helps you remove them from the container more easily. Next, place the flowers in a freezer bag or an airtight container and leave in the freezer for at least 24 hours.

2 When you're ready to make the dye, fill a non-reactive pot or bowl with warm water.

3 Take the frozen flowers out of the freezer and immediately submerge them in the warm water, before they have a chance to start defrosting.

4 Squeeze the flowers to encourage the colour to come out. You can do this for a few minutes until the water is full of colour.

5 Leave the flowers to sit in the water for a day or more to let the cold extraction continue. The flowers will continue to colour the water. Alternatively, apply gentle heat to the dye bath to encourage a quicker dye extraction process – do this for around 30 minutes, or until the water reaches a deep enough shade.

6 When you have sufficient amount of colour, strain the plant material out. To check the colour is deep enough, dip a spoon into the bowl – if it disappears, you have lots of colour.

7 Add the fabric to the dye bath and use either a cold dye method, or a hot dye method (see p58–59 and follow the guidelines below).

8 For a cold dye method just leave the fabric in the bowl until the desired colour is achieved. For a hot dye method, apply a very gentle heat for around 30 minutes, or until the fabric reaches a deep enough shade.

9 After dyeing, remove the fabric and hang it out to air dry somewhere warm and dry and out of direct sunlight for several days or weeks to cure – the longer you leave it, the better.

10 Once cured, iron with a press cloth. Then wash it with pH–neutral soap, rinse it with cool/lukewarm water and hang it out to air dry.

HAPAZOME

Hapazome is a printing technique which allows you to create unusual patterns and colour very quickly, just with the use of a mallet. Since it often uses fugitive plant colours, it's good to team it with craft projects that are less concerned with colour fastness and work well as temporary items – a beautiful gift card, for example. Or since wrapping paper is so short-lived, why not make it really biodegradable by using unbleached, recycled paper and local botanical colours?

I recommend trying this technique out on some similar scraps of cloth or paper to that of the final piece to get an idea of the best pressure and amount of hammering to use. With practice, you will get to learn how much hammering is enough or too little. You don't want to do it so much that the plant material becomes pulp and sticks to the fabric or paper. And on the other hand, you need to do it hard enough to get a good impression.

YOU WILL NEED
Plant materials (fresh petals and leaves)
Card or paper, to protect the printing material
Fabric (washed, scoured and mordanted) or recycled paper, to print on
Rubber mallet
Steam iron
Press cloth

PLANT MATERIALS My favourites to use are elegantly shaped Japanese maple and herb robert leaves, tiny violas and cute clovers – but I use whatever I find growing around me at the time. Many flowers will provide exciting bright colours, such as magenta and violet, but these colours will change and soften over time – tree mallow flowers, for example, give a gentle purple pink, which will fade away within just a few weeks. Some common and wild flower petals and seed buds are known for reliable colour, including roses, cornflower, buddleia, marigolds, chamomile, daisy, heather, hollyhock, chrysanthemums, petunias and geraniums. Experiment with other plant materials, such as berries, roots, leaves – and even waste foods, such as onion skins, carrot tops, purple cabbage ends or kale or chard leaves.

FABRIC I've used a soft woven satin silk (animal fibre) for this project as it takes up colours readily. For a similar result you can try a silk such as habotai or crêpe de chine. You can also try plant fibres, such as a finely woven linen or calico.

MORDANT If you're using silk, mordant with mineral-based mordant alum and cream of tartar, see p35. For linen or calico, use the two-step mineral-based mordant oak gall with alum and soda ash, see p38. Though the latter won't yield such bright results.

PROCESS
1 To prepare the flowers and leaves, snip the stem away from the base so you have relatively flat plant material. You can also press them with a flower press or between two heavy books.

2 Find a good strong surface to work on, such as a stone floor. Lay some card or paper down as a protective surface for the fabric or paper to go on.

3 Lay the fabric or paper down on the flat surface, and place the plant materials on top. I've created a mirror image for this project – to do this, fold the cloth or paper surface over the top of the plant material, so that you get two prints from the same items. If you don't want a mirror image, use some scrap fabric or another sheet of paper over the plant materials.

4 Using the rubber mallet, gently bash the surface until you see the colour coming through, and you feel that you have sufficiently pressed all the botanicals. Once you're happy with the design, gently shake off the plant material, or peel it off.

5 Allow the fabric to hang to air dry for a few days, out of direct sunlight. Usually, the longer you leave the cloth to cure before washing, the more substantive the colours will be.

6 As this is not the most permanent printing technique, it's a good idea to treat the prints gently after making. Steam press fabric with an iron and press cloth before washing it. Delicate hand-washing with cool water, pH-neutral soaps and air drying are a good approach to prolonging its lifetime.

Cornflower, pansy and Japanese maple on silk

INDIGO VAT DYEING

Indigo is a vat dye and unlike other natural dyes, it is not soluble in water. Instead it is soluble in an alkaline environment from which the oxygen has been removed.

Extracting indigo from its plant origin requires a complex fermentation process, which is labour and time intensive. It has to be extracted in water in its colourless 'indican' state, fermented, and finally mixed with lime and pressed into cakes.

For centuries, indigenous cultures have used a fermentation vat technique that is a very skilled art. It takes at least ten days to prepare the vat before being able to use it, and once ready it takes a very experienced dyer to keep it balanced and in a dyeable state. Any irregularities can imbalance the vat and set back the dyer several more days before dyeing can proceed again.

Thankfully a simplified method was developed by French chemist and natural dyer Michel Garcia, using a straightforward process and only three natural ingredients: slaked lime, fructose sugar and indigo. This method has been adopted by dyers around the world and is the basis of the instructions here.

Indigo has a wonderful history. The name indigo may have come from one of the oldest civilizations in the world, in the Indus Valley of India. The Greek word indikon literally translates as 'Indian dye' or 'Indian', which later became 'indigo' in English. Indigo is one of the most ancient and rare of natural dye colours – a cuneiform tablet from Mesopotamia dating back to 600 BC holds a recipe for a layered blue dye. It was used as a pigment for making paints, medicines and cosmetics by the ancient Egyptians and Romans, for medieval manuscript illuminations, and in masterpieces by artists such as Rubens during the late 16th to early 17th centuries.

Around 50 kinds of some 200 indigo-bearing plants grow in India, the earliest major centre of natural indigo production. From here it was exported in small cakes, which in 300–400 AD the Greeks and Romans believed were precious minerals.

It was not until the 13th century that Marco Polo, following his voyage to Asia, returned to enlighten those in Europe that indigo was actually a plant-based product. In the 19th century, indigo was known as 'blue gold' and was the ideal trading commodity: it travelled well and had a long lifespan, and it was compact, highly valued and rare.

Indigo refers to the dye compound contained within indigo-bearing plants. One of the most commonly used commercially for obtaining indigo dye is *Indigofera tinctoria*. Japanese indigo (*Persicaria tinctorium*) is another popular variety. In South and Central America you will find anil (*Indigofera suffruticosa*) and in Europe, our native species, although somewhat paler in colour, is woad.

Woad has a lower concentration of indigo, so local woad industries were threatened when imported indigo began to arrive from India in huge quantities. In response some governments laid down harsh rules throughout the 16th to early 17th century to outlaw the use of Asian indigo, naming it 'the devil's dye', and the 'false and pernicious Indian drug'. Indigo does have something of a dark history: the East India Company had manipulated Indian farmers into turning their land from growing food crops, which communities relied on, to growing valuable indigo crops for export. But the farmers only received a tiny 2.5% of the market value of the indigo and quickly went into debt. This led to a huge 'indigo revolt' in 1859, in which many peasants were slaughtered.

The burgeoning fashion industry of the 19th century and the Industrial Revolution, along with the popularity of Levi's jeans, demanded vast quantities of blue-dyed cloth. This spurred the development of a synthetic replacement for indigo by German chemist Adolf von Baeyer during the 1880s. Following this, both the natural indigo and woad industries collapsed. Today, only some small-scale natural indigo farming exists, for artisan natural dyers.

YOU WILL NEED
Rubber gloves, face mask and goggles
Indigo
Slaked lime (calcium hydroxide)
Fructose sugar
Scales or measuring spoons
Large bowl
Mug or old jar
Measuring cups
Heat source
Bain-marie-style bowl inside a pot
Thermometer
Long-handled spoon
Dye vat (pot)
pH-neutral soap

INDIGO When using powdered indigo, remember that it is a precious dye material, extremely valuable and rare – so be careful to avoid wasting any pigment during the dyeing process.

You can buy indigo online – look for organically grown and processed varieties. It comes as a deep blue powder and is expensive. As a rough guide, you'll need 25g (⅞oz) of indigo powder, 50g (1¾oz) of slaked lime and 75g (2⅝oz) of fructose to dye around 500g (18oz) of washed, scoured and dry fabric a medium to deep blue colour.

SLAKED LIME AND FRUCTOSE I use slaked lime (calcium hydroxide) to create the alkaline solution. Slaked lime is made when lime or quicklime (calcium oxide) is mixed, or 'slaked', with water. It has many names, including hydrated lime, caustic lime, builders' lime, slack lime or pickling lime. You can get it from builders' merchants or some DIY shops.

The slaked lime then has to be reduced, using fructose (a sugar) to remove excess oxygen from the solution. You can buy fructose (which comes as crystals) in whole food shops or some supermarkets.

FABRIC I've used a 100% organic and natural cotton (plant fibre) for this project. You can use any light or medium weight plant fibre.

MORDANT Indigo doesn't require a mordant, which saves time, energy and water in comparison to most other types of dyeing.

SAFETY Slaked lime (calcium hydroxide) is a strong alkaline, and prolonged exposure may cause severe skin irritation, chemical burns, blindness or lung damage. It's extremely important to observe the following safety instructions when preparing and using the vat.

Avoid prolonged contact with skin, splashes from getting in your eyes or swallowing any dye materials. Protect your hands with thick waterproof gloves and cover your eyes with protective goggles.

Be careful to avoid inhaling dust particles when handling powders. Wear a dust mask, and work in a well-ventilated area. Store all ingredients in clearly labelled containers, out of reach of children and pets.

If disposing of spent solutions, do so responsibly, by diluting with plenty of water and pouring onto waste land (after asking the landowner) or flushing into the sewage system.

PREPARING THE VAT

1 Measure out the required amount of indigo powder, using the measuring spoons or scales, in a ratio of 1 part indigo, 2 parts slaked lime (calcium hydroxide), 3 parts fructose. As an example, to dye 500g (18oz) of fabric to a medium to deep blue you'll need 25g (⅞oz) of indigo, 50g (1¾oz) of slaked lime and 75g (2⅝oz) of fructose.

2 For your vat, use a large steel mixing bowl, or other non-reactive container. Mix a tiny amount of warm water with the indigo powder – just enough to make a paste.

3 Using a mug or old jar, stir in 1 to 2 cups of warm water (around 43–50°C or 109–122°F) and blend to a smooth consistency. Add the fructose bit by bit, stirring it in until it has dissolved.

4 Next start to slowly add the slaked lime – a bit at a time, not all at once – stirring well and smoothing out any clumps with each addition. Note that adding the slaked lime can create heat and it has a tendency to lump together, creating more heat, so it's best to work out any clumps quickly. Adding slaked lime may also cause bubbling and overflowing, so add it gradually and with great care.

5 Once you have a smooth consistency and all the lumps have been worked out, add enough warm water to fill the vat to about 5cm (2in) below the top rim. Stir around carefully in a clockwise motion, allowing the mixture to swirl into a circular vortex and the bubbles to collect in the centre. This collection of bubbles is called the 'indigo flower'.

6 Leave the dye to settle. Once settled the indigo flower should appear blue, with no white flecks. Let it sit for 30 to 60 minutes. During this time, the liquid will start reducing: the sugar is causing a chemical reaction that causes the oxygen to leave the solution.

7 After this time, take a clean stainless steel spoon and dip below the surface of the liquid to check its colour. It should no longer appear dark blue or greeny-blue – instead, it should be a clear liquid with an amber, yellow, greeny-yellow, yellow-brown or yellow-red colour (depending on the type of indigo used). If you are using a transparent glass vat, you will see a layer of sediment on the bottom. If the liquid does not appear to be changing colour yet, but the edges of the surface appear to be a clear yellow, this is an indication that the process is happening and it just needs a little more time.

8 If it remains a thick blue colour, carefully stir again in a clockwise circular motion as before, making sure you are mixing the bottom layer of sediment with the top layer. Then stand the vat in a bain-marie or similar, and heat it up to 50–60°C (122–140°F) for 30 minutes to help the process along. Always use a bain-marie as the indigo shouldn't be heated over a direct heat at this stage.

9 The dye is ready for use when the liquid has changed colour as described in step 7, has a dark blue indigo flower on the top (the collection of bubbles on the top) and an iridescent coppery scum on the surface (a bit like a petrol spill).

10 When you feel that you have the desired result, give the mixture a careful stir and top with more hot water (50–60°C or 122–140°F), filling the vat, but leaving a few centimetres/inches at the top to allow you to submerge the fabric without the indigo spilling out. You should see it start to take on a murky yellow-green hue and within about 30 minutes it should have reduced again.

11 After this time, check to see if you have the same signals again: the blue indigo flower, the coppery scum, and a transparent yellowish liquid below the surface. Once this stage is complete, you can start the dyeing.

From top left: Adding fructose; Stirring out the lumps; Indigo 'flower'; Yellowish liquid

Bain-marie on a hot plate

DYEING

1 The vat has two layers. The upper layer is the transparent yellowish solution – this is the dye solution and is where the fabric should stay when dyeing. The bottom area is the sediment, which you need to keep separate from the dye solution. Be careful not to let the cloth go too far down into the vat, where it may touch the bottom layer of sediment. This can lead to uneven dye colouring, and encourages the sediment to mix into the upper layer of the dyeing area, which could cause the vat to unbalance – in which case you may have to go through the process of balancing it again. You could try using a plastic laundry basket inside larger vats, above the sediment and fastened to the top of the vat, to act as a protective barrier so your hands can move more freely without worrying about how deep the fabric has gone.

2 When you're ready to dye, remove the indigo flower from the surface of the vat using a spoon or sieve.

3 Keep an eye on the temperature of the vat using the thermometer, as you will want it to stay between 30–60°C (86–140°F) while dyeing. If it starts to get too hot, turn off the heat. It won't necessarily damage the indigo if it gets too hot (though it might get too hot for gloved hands). But if it's too cold, you will not be able to dye.

4 Wearing protective gloves on both hands, put the pre-wetted fabric slowly into the vat, submerging it completely in one motion. It's important that it doesn't get dipped, then come up, then go back under again, because this would introduce extra oxygen into the vat.

5 Keep the fabric submerged for about 30 seconds, massaging it to encourage the dye to enter the fibres evenly. Don't keep the fabric submerged for long periods of time – excessive dip time may mean the dye does not attach to the fabric properly, which could impact colour fastness.

6 Bring the fabric out of the vat, again all in one motion, but only to hover slightly above the surface of the liquid. This is so that any drips do not travel too far before they hit the liquid, which again reduces the amount of oxygen entering the vat.

7 Indigo dye is precious and expensive, so it's important to reduce the amount of waste at this point. With the piece of cloth still hanging in one hand above the liquid, only a few centimetres/inches above the surface, give the cloth a squeeze from top to bottom slowly so any excess dye liquid goes back into the vat. This also makes it easier for the indigo dye in the cloth to oxidise, as the oxygen can get to the fibre more easily.

8 Open up the cloth fully and watch as it turns from green to blue in front of your eyes. This is the oxidising process and the final element to the dye chemistry. Wait until the cloth is entirely blue, and no greeny areas remain, before continuing. Be particularly aware of any folds or areas that need to be opened up more fully to expose the dye to oxygen, and make sure that they have turned blue before continuing.

FURTHER DYEING

1 After the first dip, rinse the cloth in a bowl of clean water (reserve this for later rinses). If you are doing multiple dips, you'll need to rinse in this bowl after every third dip. Wring out any excess water before reintroducing the cloth to the vat.

2 Indigo is a layered dye and it will take several dips to achieve a medium to dark colour, rather than one long dip. Experiment with samples of cloth to find out how many dips, and how long the dip times need to be, to achieve the shade you want. Some very dark blues will require 15–20 dips.

3 Follow the dyeing steps again and again until you reach the shade you are after. Remember that the item will look darker when wet: after it's been washed and dried, it will be much lighter – you will get a knack for this with experience.

POST-DYEING

1 Rinse the fabric with lukewarm water, wash with pH-neutral soap, then rinse it again. Do this three times, or until the rinse water runs clean.

2 Hang out the fabric to air dry out of direct sunlight.

BALANCING THE VAT / TROUBLESHOOTING

Since indigo is not soluble in water, the amount of water used in the process is very minimal. And once in the vat, it stays there – it doesn't need to be removed as the vat can be balanced by adding more dye ingredients to allow for more dyeing. In fact, the vat lasts forever – you simply keep balancing it by topping it up with more indigo, slaked lime or fructose – or all three if needs be.

If you have followed the steps correctly, and have both an indigo flower and a coppery scum but the liquid is still dark blue, try stirring in 1 tbsp of fructose to encourage the reduction to occur and the colour to change.

If you've tried the previous suggestion and it hasn't changed colour after 30 minutes, and you still have the indigo flower and copper scum, you may need to wait longer or add more fructose. Try giving it another stir and wait 15 minutes. If this still does nothing, stir in another teaspoon of fructose.

If you have no indigo flower or coppery scum, stir in 1 tbsp of slaked lime.

If you have no indigo flower, but you do have blue bubbles and a coppery scum, this is still okay – the bubbles may just have dispersed.

If the dye liquid turns blue, it needs to be rebalanced by stirring in 1 tbsp of slaked lime and 2 tbsps of fructose and waiting 30 minutes. It should then turn a transparent yellowish colour again. If not, try applying some heat or follow the troubleshooting tips above.

If you keep dipping and see no deepening of the colour, you may have used up the indigo, so you will need to add more. Follow the ratio in step 1 to measure out the right amount for the amount of cloth. Add the extra indigo to the vat by first mixing it with water to make a paste, then a liquid, and then carefully adding that to the vat. Stir the whole vat with a long-handled spoon and wait for it to settle, before following the dyeing steps again.

INDIGO CHART

The photograph on the right shows the number of dips needed to achieve various shades of blue. The fabric is organic cotton (plant fibre). From the top:

0 DIPS
1 DIPS
3 DIPS
6 DIPS
12 DIPS
18 DIPS
24 DIPS

SHIBORI

Shibori is an ancient Japanese dyeing technique, used to create repeat patterns by compressing areas of fabric using wooden blocks, string, clamps or a range of found objects, which then prevent the dye from penetrating and therefore stop – or resist – that area of fabric from being dyed.

The name comes from the Japanese 'shiboru', which refers to a method of wringing or squeezing laundry. The earliest known example of this technique dates back to the 8th century, when the main fabrics available were only cotton, hemp and silk. Indigo was the preferred dye of choice, although there were also dyers using madder and beetroot.

There are many different shibori techniques and types of equipment, making a diverse range of designs. With arashi shibori, cloth is wrapped around a long pole and string is wound over it to create small creases, then the fabric is pushed down the pole so that it is squashed together at one end. This gives wonderful wavy water-like impressions. Itajimi shibori requires a pair of shaped objects, traditionally made from wood, which are placed on either side of a concertina-folded cloth and compressed with string to resist the dye. Kanoko shibori is what we commonly refer to as 'tie-dye' in the West – it involves binding areas with thread to create circle shapes in the cloth.

There is a correct way to use shibori techniques and precision is typically part of its tradition. However, there are a thousand ways in which you can adapt the forms and materials, and much beauty is to be found in the inconsistencies and mistakes! There are an infinite number of ways in which you can bind, fold and stitch cloth to achieve different patterns. You may find that some techniques suit certain kinds of fabric better than others, and you can also use more than one style together, to create even more intricate designs. And you can experiment with using any kind of natural dye colour. These pages demonstrate a couple of simple and elegant shibori techniques for you to try.

YOU WILL NEED

Fabric (washed, scoured and mordanted)
Steam iron
Press cloth
2 square wooden blocks
C-clamps/market clips
String
Tongs
Indigo vat or dye bath
pH-neutral soap

FABRIC I've used a 100% organic and natural cotton (plant fibre) for this project. You can use any light or medium weight, plant fibre to achieve a similar look. But you can experiment with any tightly woven animal or plant fibre.

MORDANT I've used indigo vat dyeing for this project, so no mordant was necessary. If you're using a different dye bath, then use the correct mordant for your fibre, see p32–38.

DYE If you're making a dye bath (rather than using indigo vat dyeing), opt for a good rich colour such as madder, cochineal, logwood or sappanwood.

ITAJIMI SHIBORI – SQUARE CONCERTINA

1 With this technique you fold the fabric concertina-style into a square, which will give you a design with a grid of squares. Make sure you have followed the appropriate scouring and mordanting instructions for the fabric you are working with.

2 Lay the piece of cloth out on the work surface and iron out any creases. You will be folding the fabric like an accordion or concertina and clamping the block around it to leave a small margin/border around the edge – it is this area that will be dyed. So start by placing one of the wooden blocks on one corner to gauge/measure how many folds you can make in the cloth, while still leaving a small margin around the block. If you want a really neat finish and a complete grid print (no half grids), then trim the fabric to size.

3 Concertina-fold the cloth from one end to the other, making equal-sized folds so you end up with a narrow length of folded fabric. You can give the folds a press with a steam iron, for a more immaculate finish, or leave unpressed for a more rustic look.

4 Take the long length of folded cloth and fold it in half from one end to the other.

5 Then concertina-fold it (or fold it back on itself) until you are left with a square shape. Press these folds too if you wish.

7 Place the folded square between the two wooden blocks so there is an equal margin of fabric left exposed the whole way around the blocks.

8 Position the clamp in the middle of the blocks, so that they are tightly compressing the folds.

9 Now submerge the whole thing in water and leave it to soak overnight, or for at least an hour, for pre-wetting before dyeing.

10 This project was done with indigo vat dyeing, and was dipped about 20 times. You can use any preferred dye bath. Leave the folded piece to dye in the bath using the hot or cold method that's appropriate to the fabric and dye. You may need to weigh the piece down with something heavy to stop it from floating to the top. Gently move it around every now and then, to make sure it is not touching any other surfaces, and is receiving the dye fully all over the exposed areas.

POST-DYEING

1 When you have finished dyeing, remove the fabric from the indigo vat and allow to cool. Carefully unfold the fabric and hang it out to air dry.

2 If you have used another dye bath, remove the fabric from the dye bath and allow to air dry out of direct sunlight. Leave to cure for a few days or weeks – the longer the better. After it's cured, wash the fabric with pH-neutral soap. And then finish setting the dye by giving the fabric a final steam with a steam iron and a press cloth.

3

5

ITAJIMI SHIBORI – TRIANGLE CONCERTINA

1 With this technique you fold the fabric down into a triangle, which will give you an interesting pattern of triangles and diamonds. Make sure you have followed the appropriate scouring and mordanting instructions for the fabric you are working with.

2 Lay the fabric out on the work surface and iron out any creases. Concertina-fold the fabric from one end to the other, so you end up with a narrow length of folded fabric.

3 Fold the top right corner at the end of the layered fabric down so it meets the left folded edge, creating a triangle on top and a diagonal end to the piece. Use the iron to press the edges of this triangle.

4 To create the next fold, turn the whole piece over and then fold the diagonal end up and over towards you so the first triangle you made is now on top and the end of the piece is square again.

5 Turn the whole thing over again, and this time fold the top left corner over to meet the right folded edge.

6 Repeat this process until the full length has been triangularly folded from one end to the other. Tie each of the three corners tightly with string, starting with the two end corners, and finally the middle one. Make sure the string has no chance of coming loose in the dye bath.

9 Now submerge in water and leave it to soak overnight, or for at least an hour, for pre-wetting before dyeing.

10 This project was done with indigo vat dyeing, and was dipped about 20 times. You can use any preferred dye bath. Leave the folded piece to dye in the bath using the hot or cold method that's appropriate to the fabric and dye. You may need to weigh the piece down with something heavy to stop it from floating to the top. Gently move it around every now and then, to make sure it is not touching any other surfaces, and is receiving the dye fully all over the exposed areas.

POST-DYEING

1 When you have finished dyeing, remove the fabric from the indigo vat and allow to cool. Carefully unfold the fabric and hang it out to air dry.

2 If you have used another dye bath, remove the fabric from the dye bath and allow to air dry out of direct sunlight. Leave to cure for a few days or weeks – the longer the better. After it's cured, wash the fabric with pH-neutral soap. And then finish setting the dye by giving the fabric a final steam with a steam iron and a press cloth.

2

5

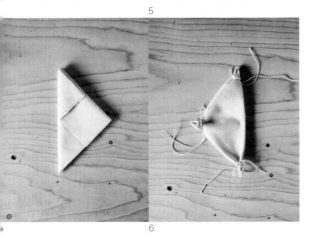

6

PRINTING INKS
FOR WOODBLOCK PRINTING AND SCREEN PRINTING

YOU WILL NEED
Plant-based binder powder – I've used gum tragacanth
Measuring cup
Bowls
Spoon
Electric blender (optional)
Extract powder – I've used logwood

EXTRACT POWDER Be aware that gum tragacanth (plant-based binder powder) has an acidic pH, which will effect the colour outcomes of your printing inks. In this case, I've used logwood (traditionally purple/blue), but after adding gum tragacanth, the resulting ink becomes orange.

PLANT-BASED BINDER POWDER You can transform natural dyes into inks suitable for screen and woodblock printing by using a plant-based binder, such as gum tragacanth, gum arabic or any other plant starch – including corn starch, potato starch, wheat starch and so on. Consider which crops grow locally that you can either extract starch from, or buy it online in powder form.

MORDANT If you are printing onto paper, it's unlikely you'll need a mordant to fix the dye colours, as colourfastness in the wash won't be an issue. Simply choose a dye that has good light-fastness and so does not fade with time. If you are printing onto fabric, you may wish to use a mordant to fix the colours well. You can pre-mordant the fabric, as usual. Alternatively, you can add the mordant (in this case alum powder) to the printing ink before using it. If you choose this option, you must work quickly and add the mordant at the last minute, as the mordant is at risk of bonding with the pigment rather than the fibre. Also, a mordanted ink can only be stored for one day.

PROCESS
For screen printing ink, use 1 tsp of plant-based binder powder to 240ml (8½ fl oz) boiling water.

For woodblock printing ink, use ½ tsp of plant-based binder powder to 240ml (8½ fl oz) boiling water

This is sufficient for several prints. Scale these quantities up to suit larger projects.

1 Measure out the required amount of plant-based binder powder and boiling water into a bowl. Mix well by hand with a spoon, or in an electric blender (that's reserved for dyeing), until all the lumps have disappeared.

2 Leave the mixture to thicken overnight in the fridge.

3 The next day, mix 1 tsp of extract powder with a few drops of hot water to make a paste, and then a few more to create a liquid consistency – use the least amount of water possible, so as not to dilute the colour too much.

4 Mix the liquid colour with 120ml (4¼ fl oz) of the binder mixture from the fridge – again you can mix by hand or by using a blender.

5 Bear in mind that colours will appear much lighter once dry and washed. For darker colours, you can use a higher ratio of extract powder to binder.

Adding a mordant to ink
First follow steps 1–5, but using different quantities. For woodblock printing ink, use 1 tsp binder to 240ml (8½ fl oz) boiling water. And for screen printing ink, use 2 tsp binder to 240ml (8½ fl oz) boiling water.

Next, make a small quantity of mordant solution using 1 tsp alum powder with the smallest amount of boiling water possible to dilute completely. Ideally only 1–2 tsp of water.

Once dissolved, add the mordant solution to the ink and blend well by hand or with electric blender.

Use this mordanted ink quickly for your printing. It's best not to store it for longer than a day.

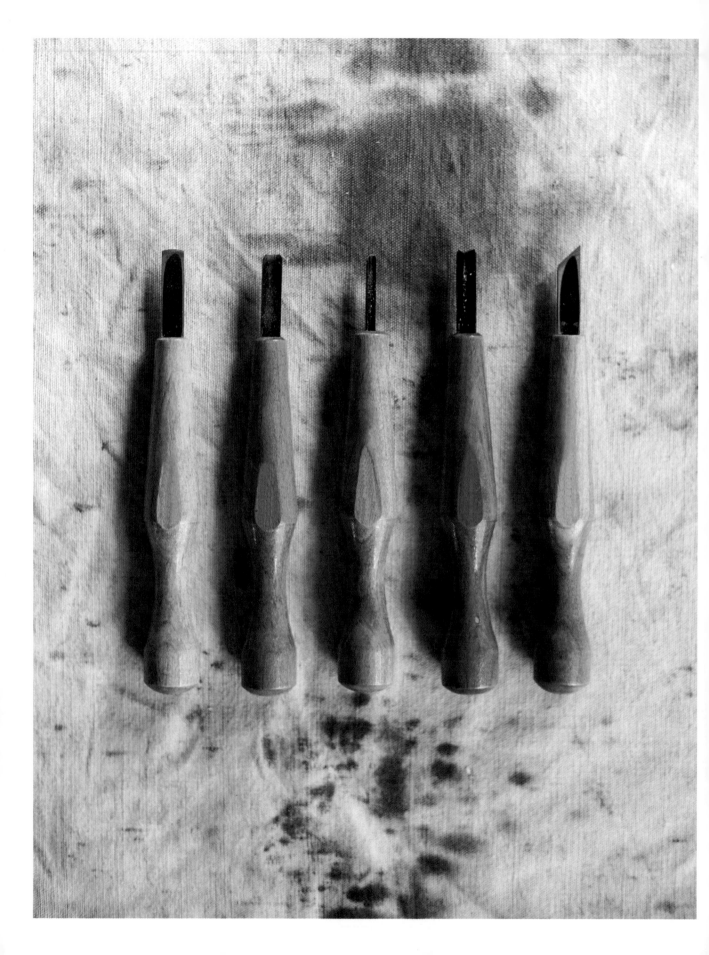

WOODBLOCK PRINTING

Woodblock printing is a traditional relief technique. It uses a wooden block with an image carved into it to apply motifs and patterns to a range of textile and paper surfaces. Tools are used to carve an image into the surface of the block, removing areas that will not be printed. The technique described in these pages uses a water-based printing ink, with a plant starch mixed into it. This is inspired by traditional Japanese and Chinese woodblock printing, which uses rice starch as a binder. This is different to that used in the similar practice of Western woodcut, which often uses oil-based inks.

Traditional Japanese woodblock printing uses thin Japanese plywood, but any local, sustainably grown softwood can be used. Pine, cedar and cypress are a bit too soft, and can compress while printing and therefore don't transfer images so well. Harder woods can be used, but they are more difficult to carve and require sharper cutting tools and consistent tool sharpening. I tend to use a cherry plywood, which has a thin layer of cherry wood on a plywood stack of birch wood, which is great for holding finely detailed designs. You can also try mahogany, poplar, ash, birch, apple or any other fruit tree.

YOU WILL NEED
Pencil and paper/tracing paper for drawing design (optional)
Woodblocks (one for each colour)
Non-slip mat or wooden bench hook
Wood block carving tools
Water mister
Inks (see recipes on p125)
Paint brush
Sponge
Paper or fabric (washed, scoured and mordanted)
Baren (for pressing with, optional)
Steaming equipment
pH-neutral soap

INK The printing ink recipe is on p125. For this project I've used logwood extract powder with gum tragacanth binder.

WOOD The wood should be clean, well seasoned or kiln dried and perfectly flat.

A thickness of ¼ inch to 3 inches works well. The thicker the wood, the less it will bend.

I would avoid using MDF (medium density fibreboard), as it contains toxic glues, with formaldehyde and other harmful chemicals, which are damaging to health when handled or inhaled while carving. They can also dull the colour of inks.

My print design has only one colour, so I only need one block. If you wish to use more colours, you will need an additional block for each colour. You can use double-sided woodblocks and have an image on each side, to minimise the amount you buy or waste.

CARVING Work on a non-slip surface or wooden bench hook that fits against the side of the work surface, to keep the block steady while you carve. Always carve away from your body. Hold the cutting tools like a pencil, and the knife with your four fingers wrapped around, and thumb on top of the upright end.

I have used Japanese wood carving tools. It's important to invest in good quality, sharp and comfortable-to-grip tools, and I find the wood-handled tools are best. The difference in using these compared to cheap plastic options is huge. You can buy them online, and they do last if you look after them. Sharpen them often, ideally after every use.

FABRIC OR PAPER I've used habotai silk (animal fibre) for this project. You can use any tightly woven animal or plant fibre.

MORDANT If you are using silk, mordant it using mineral-based mordant alum and cream of tartar, see p35. Or for the correct mordant for your fabric, see p32–38.

If you're using paper, prepare it before printing by spraying each sheet lightly using a water mister. Stack the sheets on top of each other, with a piece of dry paper above and below the stack, then wrap in a plastic bag and leave overnight. This allows the ink to be absorbed into the paper when printing.

PROCESS

1 You can draw your design directly onto the wooden block if you feel confident. If not, sketch it on some paper first, and then transfer the image using tracing paper or carbon paper.

2 Begin to cut into the block, using the knife tool first to trace the outline of the motif. The line should remain visible, as you are cutting along the side of it.

3 When you have finished cutting around the line, take the smallest gouging tool in your kit and, working close to the line, start to carve away from the knife cut. Use a shallow stroke to begin clearing the wood around the line drawing and work for a couple of strokes outwards from the line.

4 Now switch to the medium gouging tool to carve a bit further out from the line. Finally, use the largest gouging tool to carve the rest (or most) of the surface off the block, so that only the line drawing design is in relief on the board.

5 When the block is ready to use, it's good to practise your printing technique a few times on some scrap paper or cloth, to experiment with how you apply pressure, the amount of ink used and how it's loaded onto the block. This may differ with each different kind of surface you print onto.

6 Lightly mist the block with water to allow it to hold the ink. And then use the brush to load a layer of ink onto it. Make sure the ink is spread on evenly by using the brush in a forward and backward motion, so no brush marks are visible. Wipe any excess ink off the sides of the print area with a sponge to give a crisp line.

7 Take a piece of dampened paper or fabric, and lay it flat on the work surface. Place the inked-up block onto the print surface, applying light pressure and using a circular motion to rub the back of the block, but being very careful not to move it around. You may also find that a few strong taps with the fleshy side of your hand give a good effect too. If you have a baren you can use this instead, applying a light pressure in circular motions.

8 Lift the block up off the surface evenly with one hand, using the other hand to hold the cloth or paper down so that all areas of the block are lifting up at the same time.

9 You can keep on printing as many times as you like, by repeating the same process. When you reload the block with ink using the brush, be careful to wipe down the sides so there are no unwanted splodges or marks.

POST-PRINTING

1 Wash your tools with water and some pH-neutral soap and let them air dry.

2 Hang the paper or fabric to air dry on a rack, out of direct sunlight, and leave to cure for a few days, or for a couple of weeks if possible. The longer you can let the ink set in and cure, the more longevity the dye will have.

3 If you are printing onto fabric, once it's dry you will need to steam the print to set the colour. I use a bullet steamer to do this for 1 hour. If you don't have access to a bullet steamer, you can fashion a makeshift steamer out of a stainless steel pot, with a strainer inside and a lid, steaming for 1 hour. Or you can use a regular steam iron for 20 minutes at a time, until you've been steam ironing for 1 hour in total.

4 For all steaming, place the dry print onto a layer of calico and place another layer of calico fabric on top, so that it is sandwiched between the two layers. Roll up into a sausage shape and carefully place inside the steamer. The calico protects the ink from smudging and leaching onto other areas of the fabric. Calico is breathable, so allows the steam to pass through, it's also cheaper than a lot of other fabrics.

5 Hang to air dry out of direct sunlight and allow to cure for a day or so. Then press with an iron and press cloth.

6 Wash the cloth with warm water and pH-neutral soap, then air dry and press it with an iron. Any further washing should also be done in this way, to preserve the integrity of the natural dyes.

3

4

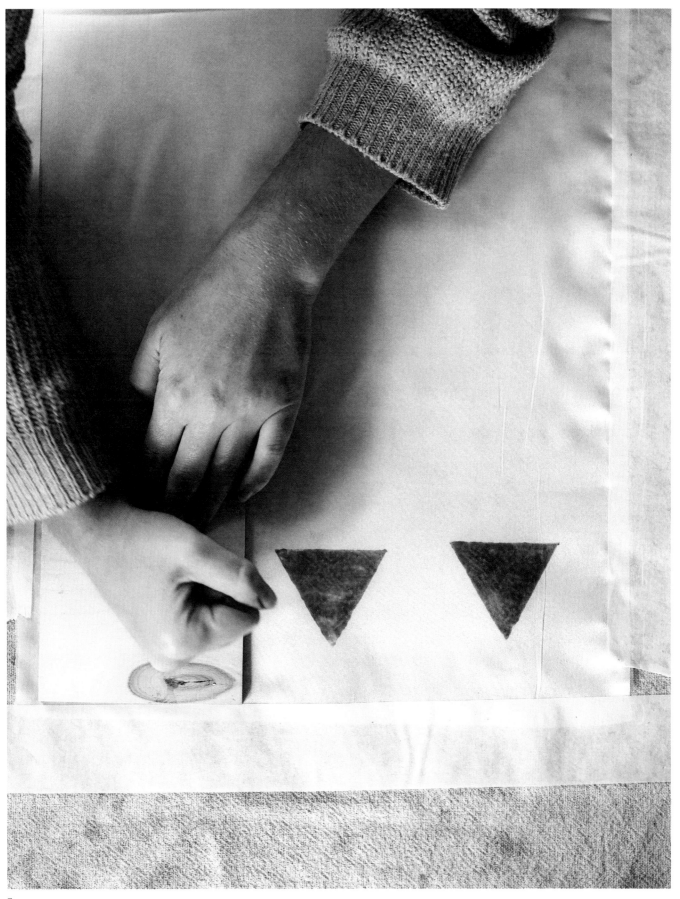

SCREEN PRINTING

Silk screen printing involves pushing ink through a screen made of fine fabric. Using paper-cut stencils to create prints gives them a unique character and simple charm.

The origins of this style of printing dates back to the Song Dynasty in China (960–1279 AD). From there, it was developed in various ways as it spread through Asia and Japan, eventually reaching Europe in the late 18th century, where it transformed into the techniques we use today.

It was around 1910 that printmakers started to experiment with synthetic light-reactive gels to expose photographic images onto screens. The technique is commonly used today to print with polyester screens (rather than the traditional silk).

Because of its ease of use, relatively cheap and accessible materials and basic equipment, this technique has been adopted as a brilliant way to print posters, flyers, T-shirts and artwork.

It's unfortunate that the mass global use of synthetic inks in modern screen printing processes has become so toxic to people and the planet. If we can return to the old ways – using natural fibre silk mesh instead of polyester, along with the organic plant-based ink recipes – we may be able to detoxify this artform.

You could experiment with making your own wooden frame, or recycle one and stretch silk mesh over it to create a biodegradable screen. And use a plant-based rubber and wooden squeegee.

YOU WILL NEED
Craft knife
Cutting mat
Fabric or paper, to print on
Masking tape
Parcel (brown) tape
Spatula
Screen printing ink (see recipe on p125)
Silk screen (43-62 threads per inch mesh-count is suitable for paper-cut stencil-printing on silk)
Squeegee (soft ones are good for silk)
Drying rack
Calico
Steaming equipment
pH-neutral soap

INK Use the recipe for printing ink on p125. For this project I've used madder with iron water added as a mordant and gum tragacanth as a binder.

PRINTING SURFACE I find that this process is much more effective if you use a padded surface on a flat table top to print onto. This can easily be fashioned using old blankets and sheets laid on top of each other.

FABRIC I recommend starting out with a soft woven silk, such as habotai, satin, crêpe de chine or charmeuse. These thin animal fibre fabrics take the colour and hold onto it particularly well. In this project, I've used organic cotton (plant fibre). But you can experiment with any tightly woven animal or plant fibre.

MORDANT I've used iron water in the printing ink as a mordant. But remember you can mordant your fabric. For the correct mordant for your fabric, see p32–38.

6 – Gliding squeegee across screen

1

3

7

The final print

PROCESS

1 Start by drawing your motif onto paper then cut it out using a craft knife and cutting mat to create a stencil.

2 Lay the fabric or paper down onto the work surface, and secure it in place with masking tape, making sure it is flat. Make sure the printing screen is clear and ready for use – check for any blocked areas.

3 The paper stencil is going to sit on top of the fabric and underneath the screen, but first you need to check the screen printing window is the correct size to fit the stencil. Do this by placing the stencil on the screen to see if it fits.

4 Lay the stencil onto the fabric and align the printing screen on top. Make sure there are no gaps around the edges of the stencil where ink may leak through. If necessary, weigh down the screen to keep it in place. Use parcel tape to block out any small gaps, or tape down paper to block out larger areas, to create the correct size or shape of the screen window to fit the stencil design.

5 Using a spatula, apply ink to the top end of the screen. Glide the squeegee from top to bottom of the screen window to flood the screen with ink.

6 Pressing down on the squeegee with a medium pressure, glide back up across the screen, carrying all the ink back to the top in one smooth move. Repeat once or twice to achieve good results.

7 Carefully lift the screen up and away from the surface, with the stencil still attached underneath, and place it somewhere safe (where the ink and stencil won't be disturbed) until you are ready to print again.

8 You can flood the screen with ink (that is, spread a thin layer of ink evenly across the screen using the squeegee), to keep it damp and stop it from blocking while you are preparing to do the next print. Don't leave it for long as it will dry and block up the screen, in which case you will have to wash and dry the screen before you can use it again.

POST-PRINTING

1 Place the printed item onto a drying rack and allow to air dry.

2 If you are printing onto fabric, once it's dry you will need to steam the print to set the colour. I use a bullet steamer to do this for 1 hour. If you don't have access to a bullet steamer, you can fashion a makeshift steamer out of a stainless steel pot, with a strainer inside and a lid, steaming for 1 hour. Or you can use a regular steam iron for 20 minutes at a time, until you've been steam ironing for 1 hour in total.

3 For all steaming, place the dry print onto a layer of calico and place another layer of calico fabric on top, so that it is sandwiched between the two layers. Roll up into a sausage shape and carefully place inside the steamer. The calico protects the ink from smudging and leaching onto other areas of the fabric. Calico is breathable, so allows the steam to pass through, it's also cheaper than a lot of other fabrics. If you have screen printed something like a T-shirt or pillowcase (with two layers of fabric), you'll need to insert calico between each layer of fabric.

4 Once you've steamed for 1 hour, remove the roll from the steamer and unroll it, taking the printed piece out of the calico layers and hanging it out to air dry.

5 Once dry, you can give the fabric a final steam press with an iron and press cloth.

6 Wash the fabric with lukewarm water and a pH-neutral soap, and air dry it again.

RESIST PRINTING

Resist printing is a continuation of the screen or woodblock printing techniques. It involves printing a design in rice flour paste – rather than a printing ink – onto fabric or paper and then either painting the ink directly onto the piece, or quickly immersing it into the dye bath. The colour permeates all but the areas blocked out with rice flour paste. Instead of printing, you can apply the paste with a paintbrush or other tool, to create different kinds of pattern. This technique is inspired by the traditional Japanese craft called katazome, which usually involves blue indigo dye applied to cotton fabrics to create inexpensive all-over patterns.

YOU WILL NEED
Organic rice flour
Spatula
Printing screen
Squeegee
Stencil
Pot of dye, suitable for cold dyeing process
Steaming equipment
pH-neutral soap

DYE I used a cochineal dye powder to make a dye bath for this project. You can use this technique with any dye material that works well with a cold dyeing method, such as madder or avocado.

FABRIC I've used a soft woven satin silk (animal fibre) for this project. For a similar result you can try a silk such as habotai or crêpe de chine. You can also try plant fibres, but the colours won't be as bright.

MORDANT If you are using silk, mordant using mineral-based mordant alum and cream of tartar, see p35. Or for the correct mordant for your fabric, see p32–38.

PROCESS
1 Begin by following steps 1 to 4 of the screen printing technique on p135; you need to create a stencil from paper and prepare the fabric and screen.

2 Make a rice flour paste by mixing 1 part organic rice flour (white or wholemeal is fine) with 2 parts water.

3 You should have a thick consistency, which is still liquid enough to pass through the print screen.

4 Using a spatula, apply paste to the top end of the screen. Glide the squeegee from top to bottom of the screen window, to flood the screen with paste.

5 Pressing down on the squeegee with a medium pressure, glide back up across the screen, carrying all the paste back to the top in one smooth move.

6 Carefully lift the screen up and away from the surface, with the stencil still attached underneath. Allow the paste to air dry on the fabric until it is solid and hard.

7 Immerse the rice flour-printed fabric into the cold dye bath and leave for about 10 seconds. Remove and air dry.

8 Repeat the dyeing process until desired depth of colour has been achieved. Alternatively, paint the dye onto the fabric with a soft brush and allow to dry between coatings.

POST-PRINTING
1 Once the desired depth of colour has been reached, leave the fabric to air dry.

2 Follow the steaming instructions in steps 2–4 in the post-printing section on p135.

3 Once dry, leave the fabric to cure out of direct sunlight for a few days, or for a couple of weeks if possible.

4 Wash the fabric with pH-neutral soap to remove the paste and any unbonded dye. Rinse it and allow it to air dry.

ART PAINTS

Paint is a substance made from a pigment and a binder, and it sits on top of a surface rather than chemically bonding with it like dyes, or burning into it like ink. You can use different binders, depending on what kind of paint you wish to make. For oil paint, you would use linseed oil. For egg tempera, you use egg yolk. Traditional watercolour paints use a water-soluble binder, much like the ink recipe on p149. You can also try experimenting with other tree resins or plant starches that are local to your area.

EGG TEMPERA Egg tempera is a permanent and fast-drying paint, made from dry colour pigments, egg yolk and water. It is very long lasting – it was used by the ancient Egyptians, Greeks and Babylonians, and up until the late 15th century by artists such as Botticelli. By the mid 1400s oil paint was being introduced, and this became the médium of choice until the 20th century, when egg tempera became popular again. Egg tempera is very stable and non-yellowing. It is a natural emulsion – a natural blend of oil and water – and water soluble, although as it dries it changes its molecular structure, so it cannot be reconstructed again by adding water. The recipe here is a for a medieval egg tempera paint, which was used before oil was available.

GOUACHE Gouache is a water-based paint, but with a more opaque consistency than watercolour: it has been in use since antiquity. It can be applied with a range of paintbrushes and reed pens, and to various surfaces. Once dry it has a matt finish and can be rewetted for continued painting.

WATERCOLOUR This type of paint is made up of pigments suspended in a water-based solution, and has a transparent quality. Watercolour painting has been practised since as far back as the cave paintings of Palaeolithic Europe. The paint can be used with reed pens, bamboo, and Chinese and Japanese calligraphy pens, and can be applied to paper, papyrus, leather, wood and canvas.

MINDFULNESS PAINTING TECHNIQUE Whether you consider yourself a painter or not, painting is a great tool for accessing untapped creativity, and opening up your creative self. Mindfulness painting is a beautiful exercise for calming the mind by slowing the breath and becoming at one with the moment, allowing your hand to guide the brush without thinking about it or controlling the outcome in any way. It can be a great means for developing intuition, dropping into a state of 'flow' and being more present in your day-to-day life.

First, get all the materials ready and to hand. Take a moment to focus on your breathing: take three deep breaths in, three deep breaths out. Allow your mind to settle, concentrating on the sensation of breath passing through the nose, in and out.

Then, when you feel grounded and out of the 'thinking' mind space, take up the paintbrush or tool and apply the paint. Become aware of the sensation of holding the brush, its texture on the skin, the feeling of dipping it in paint, the motion of air across your hands.

Allow your hand to move freely across the page, without thinking about the outcome. See where it goes naturally and allow this feeling to go on.

egg tempera paint

YOU WILL NEED

6mm (¼in) or 10mm (⅜in) thick glass or polished granite
  grinding slab or clean tile
Dye powder – I've used indigo
Palette knife
Distilled or boiled water
Glass eye-dropper
Glass muller
Fresh egg yolk
Kitchen paper
Small glass
Honey (runny)

DYE POWDER As well as indigo powder, you can use natural dye powders and extract powders such as madder, cochineal, indigo, weld, black walnut and woad. You can also use earth pigments, such as raw umber, raw sienna and yellow ochre, or other rocks and stones that you can forage.

If you are using plant material or earth pigment rocks, you will need to start by making a powder. For plant material, dry it first, and then chop it up and grind it down in a pestle and mortar, or using an electric coffee grinder. For rocks and stones, place them inside the middle of a magazine, fold it closed and then smash the outside with a hammer to get small lumps. These can then be processed in a large stone pestle and mortar fairly quickly.

GLASS MULLER AND SLAB A glass muller is a handmade weight made from glass with a smooth flat underside. It's used to grind pigment or other particles into a paint medium. It should only be used on a flat surface of tempered glass, marble or granite, such as a marble tile. You can buy both the muller and a suitable surface relatively cheaply online.

PROCESS

1 Clean the grinding surface with pH-neutral soap, water and cotton or muslin, not paper. Then dry it with a cloth. Next, put ½ tsp dye powder onto it.

2 Take the palette knife in one hand and with the other use a glass eye-dropper to add a few droplets of water onto the powder. Blend together, using a circular motion with the palette knife to work out any lumps. You're looking for a loose, smooth paste.

3 Take the glass muller and place it down on top of the mixture, moving it around in a clockwise motion to finely compress and blend the pigment and water.

4 You will feel some friction between the muller and the surface, but this will gradually ease as any tiny lumps are worked out. Keep circulating the muller until you feel that the friction has gone. You should also notice a difference in the quality of sound as you move the muller – it will become smoother and quieter.

5 Once the grinding is silent and the mixture is a smooth consistency, use the palette knife to scrape it all together into one small area.

6 Separate the egg yolk from the white by taking the yolk in your hand, and then rolling it from palm to palm allowing the white to drain through your fingers. Roll the yolk across some kitchen paper, to absorb any last amounts of white.

7 Holding the egg yolk in one hand, pierce the sac with your nails or a sharp knife, and capture the yolk inside in a small glass. Discard the egg white and yolk sac, keeping only the yolk liquid to use.

8 Pour 1 tsp of the egg yolk onto the pigment mixture and blend with the palette knife. Never grind using the muller after the egg yolk has been added, as the paint would just dry out completely and be ruined.

9 Add a few drops of honey to help preserve the paint mixture, and put it into a small dish.

USING EGG TEMPERA The paint is ready to use once you've made it up. It cannot be stored for long periods of time so should be used within three or four weeks.

The paint needs to stay wet, so it's best to keep it in foil or a foil tube to stop it from drying out. More water can be added if it begins to dry, but once it is dry it is set and will not re-wet.

When painting, build the egg tempera up in layers as it dries very quickly – within half a minute. A typical egg tempera painting has 50 to 100 layers in it.

Use a crosshatch painting technique to achieve a good result. The paint shouldn't be applied thickly as it will crack and peel.

It is best painted onto wooden boards rather than flexible canvas, as the flex in the surface may cause paint to flake off.

Sable brushes are the best choice of tool for this paint. Squirrel hair is good too, and cheaper than sable.

gouache paint

YOU WILL NEED

To scale up this recipe, use a ratio of 2 parts dye powder to 1 part binder

Dye powder
Gum arabic solution
Calcium carbonate/chalk powder (optional)
Measuring spoons
6mm (¼in) or 10mm (⅜in) thick glass or polished granite
    grinding slab or clean tile
Palette knife
Distilled or boiled water
Glass eye-dropper
Glass muller

DYE POWDER I've used madder dye powder to make this paint. Cochineal and indigo are two of the traditional dye powders you can use for good colour results.

GUM ARABIC SOLUTION This is a binder used in making some paints. You can buy gum arabic powder online or from art shops – it can come in rock form and needs to be ground into a powder before use.

To make a gum arabic solution, mix 3 parts of boiling water to 1 part of gum arabic powder. Mix this by hand, continually stirring for 10–15 minutes. Don't do this in a blender, as it tends to whip up and cause bubbles. The solution should be quite thick. To finish, weigh the solution, and add 25% of its weight in runny honey – acacia honey is ideal, as it comes from the same acacia tree as gum arabic.

PROCESS

1 Make sure the grinding surface is clean – clean it with pH-neutral soap, water and cotton or muslin, not paper. Dry it with a cloth. Measure out 2–4 tsp of dye powder onto the grinding slab – this can either be 100% powder, or 25% (1 tsp) chalk and 75% (3 tsp) powder. Chalk is a whitener and will make the paint more opaque.

2 Take the palette knife in one hand and with the other add a few drops of water onto the powder. Blend together, using a circular motion with the palette knife to work out any lumps.

3 Take the glass muller and place it down on top of the mixture, moving it around in a clockwise motion to finely compress and blend the pigment and water.

4 You will feel some friction between the muller and the surface but this will gradually ease as any tiny lumps are worked out. Keep circulating the muller until you feel that the friction has gone. You should also notice a difference in the quality of sound as you move the muller – it will become smoother and quieter.

5 Once the grinding is silent and the mixture has a smooth consistency, use the palette knife to scrape it all together into one small area.

6 Add 1–2 tsp gum arabic solution and mix well with the palette knife.

7 Put into a small dish ready to use or store.

USING GOUACHE You can add a couple of drops of vodka, essential oil or clove oil to extend the life of the paint. It will usually keep in the fridge for up to 2 or 3 months.

Once used and dried on a surface, the paint will stay colourfast and not go mouldy.

Gouache doesn't require a sealant, although a varnish can be used over the top.

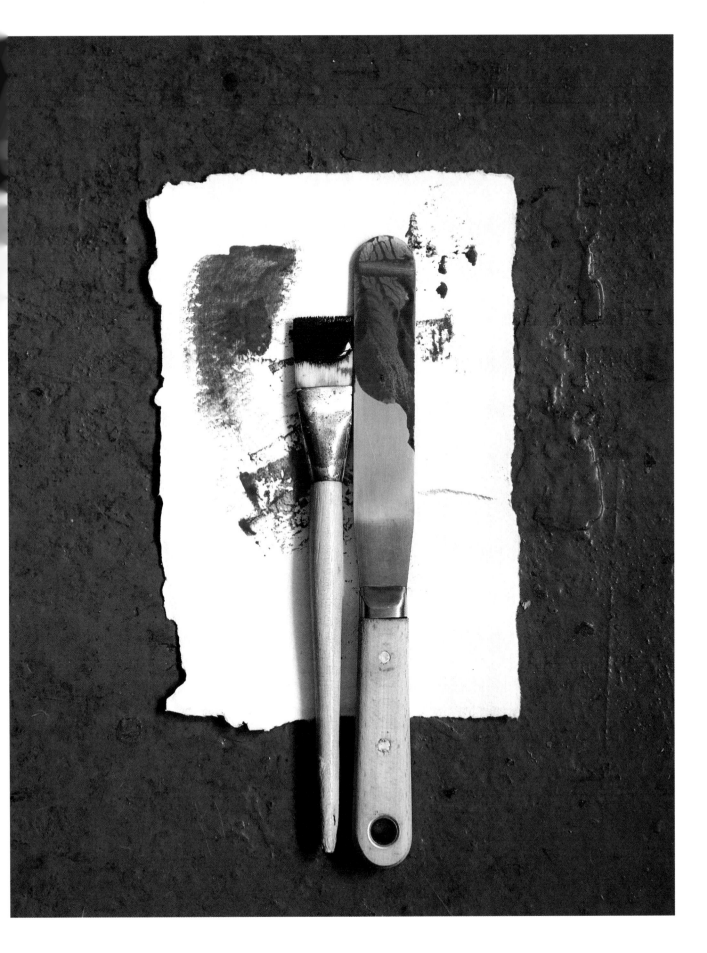

watercolour paint

YOU WILL NEED

To scale up this recipe, use a ratio of 1 part dye powder to 1½ parts gum arabic binder

Dye powder – I've used fustic
Gum arabic solution (see p144)
Measuring spoons
6mm (¼in) or 10mm (⅜in) thick glass or polished granite grinding slab or clean tile
Glass muller
Palette knife

PROCESS

1 Clean the grinding surface with pH-neutral soap, water and cotton or muslin, not paper. Dry it with a cloth. Measure out 1 tsp of dye powder onto the grinding slab. Take the palette knife in one hand and with the other add a few drops of the gum arabic solution at a time, no more than about 1½ tsp in total. Blend together, using a circular motion with the palette knife to work out any lumps.

2 Take the glass muller and place it down on top of the mixture, moving it around in a clockwise motion to finely compress and blend the pigment and solution.

3 You will feel some friction between the muller and the surface but this will gradually ease as any tiny lumps are worked out. Keep circulating the muller until you feel that the friction has gone. You should also notice a difference in the quality of sound as you move the muller – it will become smoother and quieter.

4 Once the grinding is silent and the mixture has a smooth consistency, use the palette knife to scrape it all together into one small area.

5 Put into a small dish ready to use or store.

USING WATERCOLOUR Red sable and kolinsky sable brushes hold a good point – ideal for watercolour.

To store, use a specialist watercolour paint tray, which has small indentations in it. The paint goes in and dries into solid tablets. These trays come in a sealable tin box which will keep the paint safe and dry.

Alternatively, you could recycle any tiny, single-portion glass jam jars to create makeshift watercolour storage. Only very small amounts of paint are required to make your own watercolour paints, so remember to use small quantities, and small storage options.

DRAWING INK

When I think of natural drawing ink, my mind wanders to medieval Britain, to old parchment paper and wax sealed scrolls, to secret messages, Robin Hood and letters between Shakespearean star-crossed lovers. It's easy to make and could bring a touch of romance to your drawing and letter writing.

The word ink is derived from the Latin *encaustus*, which literally means 'burned in'. The tannic acid used in traditional ink recipes actually burns the top layer of the paper or parchment when it is applied, while the pigment sits on top of the surface layer, much like a paint. There are countless recipes for making ink, which may be adapted and added to as you go, to adjust to differences in surface qualities and textures.

I've given two recipes for you to try. One is a simple ink recipe, which you can use with many substantive dye plant materials to create a range of colourful inks. The other is a traditional indelible ink recipe, which contains iron to deepen the colours and give black hues, and leave a permanent mark. It's an oak gall ink, which would once have been used with a quill, or later a dipping pen. It can still be seen on historical manuscripts, though some have suffered damage due to the acidity of the tannic acid in the oak galls, which over time eats away at natural fibres such as paper or parchment.

You can use these inks for drawing with a quill or dipping pen, or any other kind of writing tool such as sticks or brushes.

BINDERS AND INKS Both inks use a binder to thicken the ink and make it suitable for writing or drawing with. In these recipes, I use gum arabic, which is a natural resin extracted from the acacia tree that is solid and translucent orange in colour. It aids the consistency of the ink, acting as a binder and creating an even dispersion of pigment.

Depending on the drawing tool, surface material and work surface, you may wish to adapt the ink and vary the type and quantity of binder to suit your needs. The paper you are writing on, the work surface it is resting on and the tool you use to draw with can all alter the way in which the ink flows from pen to paper.

You can experiment with a few different options for binder paste to see which works best with your choice of plant colour. Egg white, oils, potato, wheat or cornflour (cornstarch), and even honey are good options.

simple drawing ink

YOU WILL NEED
Dye powder or plant material
Measuring cup or spoons
Gum arabic solution (see p144)
Salt
Vinegar

Additional items for plant material process
Scales
Heat source (optional)
Pot
Sieve

DYE POWDER OR PLANT MATERIAL This process begins with extracting colour from local, seasonal plants and waste foods to create a dye bath with the smallest amount of water possible, and then reducing this down to a concentrate. Mix in a binder and a preservative to make an ink.

I've used cochineal dye powder, but you can use any fresh, dry or frozen plant materials, or other dye powders. You can use materials such as chopped beetroot, avocado rinds, coffee grounds, tea leaves, berries, eucalyptus, nettle leaves, dock or dandelion root or any other dye plant.

PROCESS: POWDER
1 Mix 1 tsp dye powder with about 2 tsp water – you want to make a paste with the smallest amount of water possible.

2 Add 1 tsp of the gum arabic solution to the paste.

3 To preserve the ink, add 1 tsp clear white vinegar and 1 tsp salt.

PROCESS: PLANT MATERIAL
1 Place 500g (18oz) of plant material (such as nettle) in a pot and add 500ml (1 pint) of water, or enough water to just cover the plant material. It's key to use the smallest amount of water possible.

2 For a quick hot extraction technique, apply heat and bring to a gentle simmer. Simmer for 30 minutes to an hour.

3 For a more environmentally friendly cold extraction technique, cover the pot with a lid and leave for several weeks, or until the water has turned dark with colour.

4 For both options, once you have a good amount of colour in the water, strain the dye bath with a sieve to remove the plant material.

5 Place the pot over a low heat, and reduce the liquid until you have a thick, syrup-like consistency and the colour saturation you prefer.

6 Add 1 tsp of gum arabic solution to your dye mixture.

7 To preserve the ink, add 1 tsp clear white vinegar and 1 tsp salt.

indelible drawing ink

YOU WILL NEED
This recipe makes about 500ml (1 pint) of ink

56g (2oz) whole oak galls, or oak gall powder
Pestle and mortar/hammer (optional)
Grinder (optional)
Scales
Rain water or distilled water
Cheesecloth
30g (1oz) ferrous sulphate powder
15g (½oz) gum arabic solution (see p144)
Ink well, for storage

OAK GALL While oak gall was the ingredient of choice in old European inks, walnut was also used, so that can be used as an alternative in this recipe to create a brown/black ink. For more on oak galls, see p37.

FERROUS SULPHATE Also known as copperas or green vitriol, is a synthesised metallic salt that can either be obtained as blue-green crystals, or in its white powder form.

PROCESS
1 Crush the dried oak galls with a pestle and mortar – or by keeping them in a drying bag and crushing them with a hammer – until you have very small lumps. Then grind to a powder using a grinder. If you've bought oak gall powder, skip straight to the next step.

2 Add 56g (2oz) of oak gall powder to 500ml (1 pint) water. Leave to soak for 24 hours.

3 Strain the oak gall liquid through the cheesecloth.

4 Mix the ferrous sulphate into the strained solution.

5 Finally, add the gum arabic solution and stir well.

6 Store in a glass ink well with a cork stopper – this will not only make it look good, but will keep it fresh and safe. Storing it in the fridge will give it an even longer life.

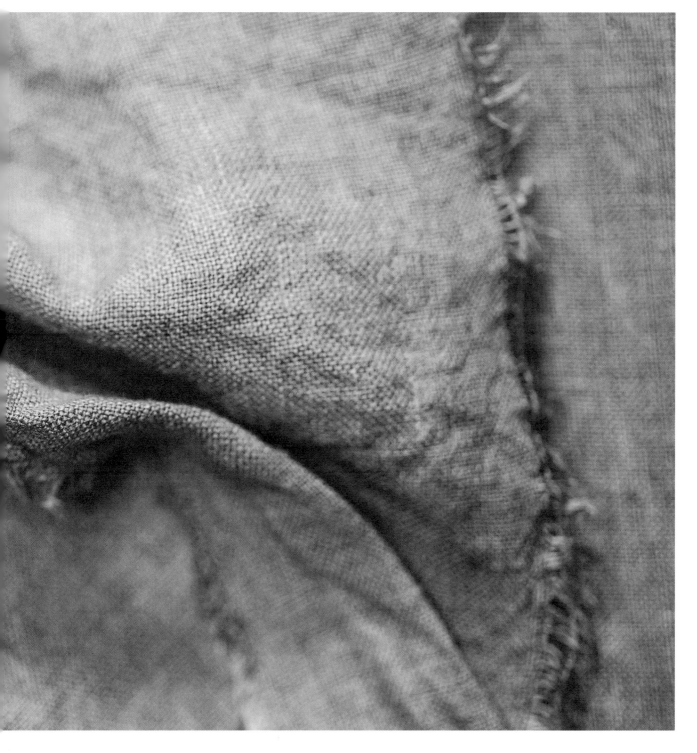

TABLE LINEN

There's something special about using food waste to make beautiful, decorative table linen – and it's a great conversational piece when you gather around the table with friends.

Consider the range of colours you can create: rich bronze from onion skins, soft dusty pinks from avocado rind and pit, purple from red cabbage ends, yellow from carrot tops, and an array of beige and greens from coffee grounds or various types of tea leaves.

Lengths of yellow onion-dyed linen, with soft edges, add a touch of romantic style. I love the rustic, crumpled look of freshly washed linen, but you can try any natural fabrics for making runners and napkins. You might also like to use larger swathes of fabric to make a full tablecloth or bed throw. Layer up different qualities of linen, from light, loose weave to thicker, heavier weights.

YOU WILL NEED
Tape measure
Dyed fabric
Fabric scissors
Iron and ironing board
Dressmaker's pins
Sewing machine
Sewing thread

DYE MATERIAL Onion skins, see p79. You'll need 100% of the weight of the washed, scoured and dried fabric in skins – so for 500g (18oz) of fabric, you'll need 500g (18oz) of dry onion skins

FABRIC Irish linen (plant fibre). You can also use organic cotton, which would give a similar rustic finish. Or silk (animal fibre) is wonderful for a more romantic look

MORDANT For Irish linen, use two-step mineral mordant, oak gall, alum and soda ash, see p38

DYE METHOD Dye bath, hot dyeing method, see p79. For a similar shade, leave the fabric in the dye bath on a simmer for 1 hour. Then take off the heat and leave in the dye bath overnight

MODIFIER I haven't used a modifier in this project, but an acidic modifier such as lemon juice or light vinegar will give brighter hues

Measure the table width or length, depending on where you want the runner to sit. A table runner looks good when it's about one third of the width of the table, and running down the middle lengthways. So if the table is 120cm (48in) wide, the runner should be 40cm (16in) wide. If you want to leave the runner in place for dinner parties, make sure there is enough space on each side of it for placemats, without them overlapping the runner.

The length of the runner should overhang the ends of the table by about 15–25cm (6–10in) on each end. So, if the table is 175cm (70in) long, the table runner will be 190–200cm (75–80in) long.

Napkins are square, and can be any size from 40 x 40cm (16 x 16in) to 50 x 50cm (20 x 20in). Larger sizes tend to be for formal events, to be folded into shapes or around silverware.

When you've established what sizes you need, cut all the pieces from the fabric. I've left a rough, frayed hem as I like the rustic look. If you would like a neater finish, allow 2cm (¾in) extra all round each piece for a hem.

Make a double hem by folding the edges of each piece under by 1cm (⅜in) to the wrong side and then fold under again by 1cm (⅜in). Press the folds with the iron and then pin into place, placing the pins at a right angle to the edge so that the needle can sew over them.

Using the sewing machine, sew the hem in place all round the edges, close to the first fold.

You could create a more elaborate design by using shibori dyeing techniques to add pattern to the cloth. For more on this, see p119.

SILK SLIP

Upcycle a vintage silk slip or camisole with fresh, dried or frozen flowers, to create a beautiful, luxurious, bundle-dyed garment. This one has been infused with herbs that offer relaxing and restorative qualities and aid female health. Delicate bursts of colour create a meaningful item to sleep in at night.

YOU WILL NEED

Silk slip
Clear vinegar
Mister bottle
Dye material
String
Steaming equipment
Tongs
Heat source
Press cloth
Steam iron and ironing board
pH-neutral soap

DYE MATERIAL Fresh and dry plants and herbs, including mugwort, lavender, rose, nettle, apple leaf, chamomile, dandelion, lady's mantle, motherwort, red clover, comfrey, raspberry leaf, violet or yarrow. Dye powder or extract powder, including sappanwood and logwood

FABRIC 100% silk vintage slip (satin silk). Try any silk item – a dressing gown, kimono, scarf or vest. Or experiment with another animal fibre, such as wool or cashmere. Make sure the fabric is still wet from mordanting, or pre-wet (see p30) the fabric before beginning

MORDANT Mineral-based mordant alum and cream of tartar, see p35

DYE METHOD Bundle dyeing, see p94–101

MODIFIER Dipped in an alkaline modifier iron solution for muted tones, see p42–43

While it is still damp (from mordanting or pre-wetting), lay the camisole out on the work surface – you may need to lay down a protective cover first. Spray the camisole all over with vinegar.

You are going to work on one half of the front of the camisole to give the final piece a mirror-image print. Find the vertical centre line and work on the right-hand side only. Scatter plant material over the right-hand front of the camisole, then very lightly sprinkle dustings of dye powder. Note that it doesn't take much of these strong powders to create a big burst of colour! Spray the plant materials and dye powders with vinegar so they are wet, too.

Make sure that the centre fold area has plant and dye material touching it the whole way down, so you don't get a blank strip all down the middle. Also try to ensure that you have plant and dye materials coming right up to the edges all round, so you don't get a blank border. Now fold the left-hand side of the camisole over, laying it perfectly on top of the right-hand side so the side edges are aligned.

Once folded, roll up the item from top to bottom, to create a sausage shape. Secure this very tightly with string – you should not be able to get your fingers underneath the string.

Add the bundle to the steamer and steam for one hour, see p46. Turn the bundle upside down every 15 minutes for even steaming results. Once an hour has passed, turn off the heat and allow to cool down. Use the tongs to remove the bundle.

When the bundle is cool enough to handle, untie the string, reserving it for future bundle-dyeing projects. Open up the bundle and shake off the plant materials. At this stage, you can dip your fabric into the alkaline modifier to mute the colours.

Hang the camisole to air dry somewhere warm and out of direct sunlight. You'll need to leave it for at least 2 weeks to allow the dyes to cure and fully set into the fabric.

After the curing process, you can use a press cloth and steam iron to give the camisole a final steam press before washing it. This is the final stage of setting the colour into the fabric.

Wash the camisole gently by hand with pH-neutral soap and warm/cool water. Rinse it with water and hang it out to air dry.

DIP-DYE GIFT TAGS

One of the simplest ways to add a touch of natural colour to gifts is with pretty dip-dyed paper luggage labels or gift tags. You can do this any time you have a dye bath left over from another project. And you can also experiment with dyeing wrapping paper or greetings cards, to which you can add a woodblock print (see p127) or write your message in drawing inks (see p148–153) for a completely natural-dyed gift wrap.

YOU WILL NEED
Dye material
Recycled paper tags
Small bowl
Water
Length of string
Pegs/hooks

DYE MATERIAL Cochineal powder, see p71. About ¼ tsp of dye powder in a small bowl of water will be enough for about 20 tags. Or use any dye bath solution leftover from another project

PAPER TAGS Paper luggage labels or gift tags, ideally recycled. You can also try recycled paper, such as Khadi paper from India, which is made from offcuts from the cotton textile industry – it has a brilliant texture

DYE METHOD Dye bath, cold dyeing method, see p58

Dip each tag into the dye bath until you get the desired depth of colour – the ones shown here only took around 30 seconds. But if you're using very robust tags, you can leave them in for as long as 12 hours if you prefer deeper shades.

Gently lift the dyed tags out of the dye bath and dip them very quickly and briefly into a bath of clear water to rinse off any excess dye sitting on the surface. This leaves behind only the true colour that has dyed the paper fibres.

Using pegs or hooks, attach the tags to a line of string to air dry. Be careful when handling them, as they are particularly fragile when wet, and the colours could smudge onto other surfaces.

Leave for 30 minutes, or until the tags are dry to the touch. For a deeper colour, repeat the process.

DARNED JUMPER

Everyone has a jumper in need of some love and restoration. A great way to extend the life of an old, moth-eaten garment is to darn it with a contrasting colour of woollen yarn to make a feature of its imperfections. This project is based on the Japanese aesthetic wabi-sabi, which celebrates beauty that is 'imperfect, impermanent, and incomplete'.

YOU WILL NEED

Jumper
Darning mushroom, or teacup (optional)
Dyed yarn
Large-eye darning needle

DYE MATERIAL Madder powder, see p73. You'll need about 10% of the weight of yarn in powder – so for around 200g (7oz) of yarn, you'll need 20g (½oz) of madder powder

WOOL Skein of yarn (animal fibre). I used a two-ply, 100% pure lambswool – but any wool is fine

MORDANT Mineral-based mordant alum and cream of tartar, see p35

DYE METHOD Dye bath, hot dyeing method, see p73. Only heat to 80°C (175°F) to avoid damaging the wool

If you are using one, place the darning mushroom, or teacup, inside the jumper under the hole.

Cut a length of yarn and thread into the darning needle. Secure the thread end by sewing a few small stitches on top of each other, close to the hole but in an area that is not damaged.

Make a line of running stitches around the outside of the hole in a loop, sewing where the fabric is not damaged.

Next make a series of vertical stitches from the top to the bottom of the loop of running stitches.

Bring the thread up at the bottom of one side and work horizontally across the vertical stitches, weaving over and under the threads of the vertical stitches.

Make a tiny stitch in the undamaged fabric next to the vertical stitches. Work a second horizontal stitch close to the first one, weaving under and over the vertical stitches in opposite way to the first horizontal strand. Make a tiny stitch in the undamaged fabric as before. Carry on working the alternate weaving sequences until you've worked over the area of the loop.

Finish by securing the thread with several small stitches in one place, weave the end through the darned area and trim off close to the surface.

CUSHION COVER

These scatter cushions are a great way to add natural colour to your home – contrasting bright dye colours and sharp geometric shapes give them a contemporary feel.

YOU WILL NEED

Paper and pencil
30 x 30cm (12 x 12in) duck/goose feather
    or down cushion pad
Tape measure or ruler
Pieces of dyed fabric
Dressmaker's pins
Dressmaker's chalk
Fabric scissors
Sewing machine
Sewing threads in suitable colours
Iron and ironing board
2 pieces of plain cotton fabric, each
    32 x 22cm (12½ x 8½in)

DYE MATERIAL The pink is cochineal, see p71. The coral is madder, see p72. The purple is logwood, see p90

FABRIC Organic cotton (plant fibre) – use a medium to heavyweight cotton with a tight weave. You could also use another plant fibre, such as linen. The project is ideal for using up scraps and offcuts

MORDANT For cotton, use two-step mineral mordant, oak gall, alum and soda ash, see p38

DYE METHOD Dye bath, hot dyeing method. For cochineal, see p71. For madder, see p72. For logwood, see p90

Draw a 32 x 32cm (12½ x 12½in) square on the paper; this includes 1cm (⅜in) all round for the seam allowance. Draw a simple geometric design using squares and triangles to fill the square.

Cut out the paper shapes and place them on the fabrics, pinning them down with some space between each one. Using the dressmaker's chalk or washable marker, mark a 1cm (⅜in) seam allowance around the whole of each shape, using a dotted line.

Cut out the fabric shapes out along the dotted lines. Use the iron to steam press the seam allowance to the wrong side all round each piece.

Arrange the fabric pieces into their correct positions, to see which ones need sewing together. Take two of the pieces and place them right sides together, with the edge to be sewn aligned. Use the sewing machine to sew a straight line along the pressed line. Press the seam open to reduce any bulkiness. Add the next pieces in the same way, until all the pieces are sewn together to create a full square.

Now make the envelope back for the cushion. On one long edge of each plain piece of fabric, fold under 3mm (⅛in), then fold under 7mm (¼in) to make a double hem. Use the sewing machine to sew each hem in place close to the first fold.

Now place one back piece flat and right side up, and add the second piece on top, also right side up, with the hemmed edges overlapping. Adjust the overlap to make the pieces into a 32 x 32cm (12½ x 12½in) square, then pin the two pieces securely together through the overlapping section.

Place the patchwork piece and the back piece right sides together, with the edges aligned all round, and pin the layers together. Place the pins at a right angle to the edge so that the needle can sew over them.

Use the sewing machine to sew all round the edge, taking a 1cm (⅜in) seam allowance all round. It's best to start in the middle of one side, sew to the corner, then pivot the piece on the needle so you can sew the next side – this gives a neat square corner. Repeat until you are back where you started, then backstitch for 2cm (¾in) to secure the end of the seam.

Remove the pins, turn the cushion cover right-side out and use something blunt to push out the corners into neat points. Press with the iron and insert the cushion pad to finish.

APRON

An indigo vat-dyed linen apron is the ideal thing to wear during other natural dyeing projects. The deep blue shade conceals all kinds of splashes and spills, and keeps its colour well through repeated washing. It's also incredibly simple to make!

I love to romanticise about the indigo kimonos of ancient Japanese soldiers who wore their handmade robes believing in their mystical protection and strength.

YOU WILL NEED

An apron template (this is available to download at botanicalinks.com)
Roll of pattern making paper
Pencil
Tape measure
Scissors
1m (1yd) of 90cm (36in) wide indigo-dyed linen
Pins
Iron and ironing board
Sewing machine
Sewing thread
3m (3yd) of organic cotton webbing, 38mm (1½in) wide

DYE MATERIAL Indigo, see p110–116

FABRIC I've used a medium to heavyweight cotton (plant fibre) with a tight weave, you could also use something similar, such as linen

DYE METHOD Indigo vat dyeing, see p110–116

First make a pattern, or use the template. To make a pattern, cut a 1m (1yd) length from the roll of pattern paper. Fold it in half, with the fold on the right-hand edge. Measure 90cm (36in) from the bottom edge vertically along the fold line and make mark 1.

From mark 1, draw a horizontal line measuring 15cm (6in) to the left, making sure it's at a right angle to the fold. The left-hand end of this line is mark 2.

Measure 35cm (14in) from the fold to the left along the bottom edge, and make mark 3.

From mark 1 measure 26cm (10½in) down the fold and make a dot. From this dot, draw a 35cm (14in) horizontal line at a right angle to the fold. The left-hand end of this line is mark 4.

Join marks 3 and 4 with a vertical line. Join marks 4 and 2 with an inward curving line.

Cut out the shape and pin it to the fabric. Cut the shape from the fabric.

Cut a 15cm (6in) square from a spare piece of fabric for the pocket.

Make a double hem by folding under the top of the pocket by 1cm (⅜in) and then fold it under again by 1cm (⅜in). Press the folds with the iron then sew the hem in place close to the first fold.

Fold under the other three sides of the pocket by 1cm (⅜in) and press with the iron.

Pin the pocket right side up and centred on the right side of the apron, 36cm (14½in) down from the top edge of the apron.

Sew around the sides and bottom of the pocket only, leaving the top open.

Make a double hem all round the apron by folding under 1cm (⅜in)

and then fold under again by 1cm (⅜in). Press the folds with the iron then sew the hem in place close to the first fold.

Cut 55cm (22in) from the cotton webbing for the neck loop.

Place the apron right-side down on the work surface, and pin the loop of webbing at the top so that each end overlaps the top hem by about 4cm (1½in) and is about 1cm (⅜in) in from each side.

Sew round in a square through the overlap at one end of the webbing, then stitch from opposite corners of the square in a cross. Repeat on the other end of the webbing.

Cut the remaining cotton webbing in half and double hem one end of each piece.

Pin the un-hemmed end of each piece on either side of the apron at the corner of the extended waistline, overlapping the side hem by about 4cm (1½in), and about 1cm (⅜in) down from the top edge.

Sew round in a square through the overlap as before, then make a cross from corner to corner.

SILK SCARF

There's something really luxurious about wrapping yourself in a beautiful silk scarf. For special occasions, it feels divine to be cloaked in a huge swath of natural cloth embellished with botanical prints, and be safely held by the sacred healing herbs printed on it.

YOU WILL NEED
2m x 1m (80 x 40in) of bundle-dyed
   silk fabric
Iron
Fine sewing needle
Sewing thread

DYE MATERIAL Fresh hollyhock and hydrangea, dry cornflower and marigold, madder, mixture of fresh and dry red rose. Dye powders cochineal and logwood

FABRIC I've used a fine pashmina-type silk (animal fibre), but you can use any tightly woven animal fibre

MORDANT For silk, use mineral-based mordant alum and cream of tartar, see p35

DYE METHOD Bundle dyeing, see p94–101

To create this particular design, I used a concertina folding technique, taking the short length of the cloth and folding it backwards and forwards, in a fan style, across the longer length of the cloth. I was left with a long, narrow, folded piece of fabric, which I then concertina-folded again in the same way as before

MODIFIER Dipped in an alkaline modifier iron solution for muted tones, see p42–43

Roll hemming works wonderfully on any kind of lightweight fabric, but not so well on heavier fabrics. It takes a while to do, especially on a large scarf such as this one, but it's worth the effort for the finished look. You can use a rolled-hem or walking foot on a sewing machine to create the hem, but I find a hand-rolled hem gives a better result.

Lay the fabric out flat on the work surface or an ironing board and press any creases out with the iron.

To make the rolled hem, begin by pressing 1.7cm (⅝in) to the wrong side all around the piece. Then fold the raw edge of the fabric under by 7mm (¼in), and you have a 1cm (⅜in)-wide double hem. Press the folds with the iron – this makes for tidy stitching and a much easier process.

Next, starting at a corner, secure the thread with a few tiny stitches in one place (rather than making a knot in the end of the thread).

Use a simple slip stitch: make a small diagonal stitch just below the bottom of the fold and then, moving diagonally from right to left, make a small stitch in the top of the fold.

Leaving a gap of about 2cm (¾in) to the left, make the next stitch, again just below the bottom fold and again moving diagonally to make a little stitch in the top of the fold. This process can be repeated three to five times before you pull the thread through.

Then gently pull the thread so that it's not too tight and pulls on the fabric, but not too loose so that there are gaps showing in the stitching. Carry on like this until you reach a corner, then secure the thread with another couple of tiny stitches, run the needle through the fold to lose the end and cut the thread close to the fabric.

Begin again with a new piece of thread, making the initial securing stitches in the corner where they can easily be concealed. Repeat until all four sides of the scarf are hemmed.

FUROSHIKI

Furoshiki is a traditional Japanese wrapping cloth that often uses indigo shibori techniques. It's much more environmentally friendly than single-use, throwaway wrapping paper, and also becomes an additional part of the gift, because the wrapping is a beautiful length of fabric that can be used again and again. It is a gift that keeps on giving.

There are numerous furoshiki wrapping techniques used in Japan, which differ depending on the item you wish to wrap, but these two simple methods will get you started.

YOU WILL NEED
A rectangular or square piece of shibori-dyed organic cotton, linen or other medium to heavyweight tightly woven cloth
Presents to wrap, square- or bottle-shaped

DYE MATERIAL Indigo, see p110–116. But you can also try this with dye powders such as madder (see p73), cochineal (see p71) or logwood (see p90)

FABRIC Organic medium-weight cotton (plant fibre)

MORDANT This project uses indigo vat dyeing, so a mordant hasn't been used. If you're using a dye bath, and would like bright colours, pair with the mordant that best suits the fibre you're using

DYE METHOD Indigo vat dyeing, see p110–116. But you can use any dye bath method. Use the shibori square and triangle accordion folds techniques, see p119–122

How to wrap a rectangular or square item
Lay the piece of cloth out flat in front of you, with one corner pointing towards you.

Place the square or rectangular item diagonally in the centre, so that the straight edges face the corners of the cloth, and you have a straight edge facing you.

Take the right-hand corner of the cloth and fold it over the item, then tuck it underneath the item.

Take the left-hand corner of the cloth and fold it over the item away from you, tucking it underneath.

Bring the two free corners together on top of the wrapped package and tie them together in a knot.

How to wrap a bottle
Lay the piece of cloth out so there's a straight side in front of you. Place the bottle upright in the centre.

Pick up the corners on the side of the cloth furthest away from you, and fold the edge between them over by about 5cm (2in). Wrap the two corners around the front of the bottle, one over the other.

Pick up the other two corners closest to you, and fold the edge between them over by about 5cm (2in).

Stretch these two corners out and around the back of the bottle, cross them over each other, bring them right around to the front again, and tie them together in a knot.

SLEEP MASK

Certain botanicals are known for their soothing and calming effects on the body and mind, and can be ideal for a sleep mask. Silk is a great fabric to use, as it feels so soft against the sensitive skin of your face. You can use a sewing machine if you prefer, although you may find it easier to sew the mask by hand, as it's quite a small item. The ribbon ties should be long enough to tie into a bow.

YOU WILL NEED

A sleep mask template (this is available to download at botanicalinks.com)
Tracing paper and pencil
Roughly 30 x 30cm (12 x 12in) of bundle-dyed fabric
Dressmaker's pins
Fabric scissors
Wool fleece (or other natural fibre wadding)
2 ribbons, each about 45cm (18in) long (or you can cut your own ribbons from the dyed fabric)
Iron and ironing board
Ruler
Chalk marker
Fine sewing needle
Sewing thread
Sewing machine with walking foot (optional)

DYE MATERIAL Fresh lavender, rose and mugwort, and dried chamomile, marigold and damiana to encourage restful sleep and sweet dreams

FABRIC Silk – this project is ideal if you have an offcut from another project

MORDANT For silk, use mineral-based mordant alum and cream of tartar, see p35

DYE METHOD Bundle dyeing, see p94–101

Trace the template onto the paper twice and cut out the shapes using paper scissors. Hold one up to your face to check the size – although bear in mind it has a 1cm (⅜in) seam allowance all round. If you want to make the mask larger or smaller, adjust the paper patterns before going any further.

You'll need to align the top edge of each pattern piece with the weft of the fabric (so, at right angles to the selvedge edge) – this will allow the mask to sit comfortably on the contours of your head. Once you are happy with their position, pin both paper patterns to the fabric with dressmaking pins. Cut around them with fabric scissors. You will also need a layer of inner padding, so use one of the paper patterns to cut the shape from the wool fleece wadding.

Lay the three mask pieces on top of each other, with the fleece in the middle, and with both fabric pieces right side outwards.

Cut a binding strip from the fabric, 3cm (1¼in) wide and long enough to go all around the outside edge of the mask. Fold the strip in half lengthways with the wrong sides together, and press all the way down the centre fold with the iron. Open out again then press each long edge to the middle crease.

Pin one end of a ribbon in place on either side of the back of the mask, so they sit level with each other, slightly above the middle point. Mark the 1cm (⅜in) seam allowance with a dotted line all round the mask on both sides, using a ruler and chalk.

Open out one side of the binding and place it right sides together onto the back of the mask, with the raw edges of mask and binding aligned. Starting at one of the sides where a ribbon is pinned, smooth the binding into place around the edge of the mask, pinning it in place as you go. Use the dotted seamline on the mask as a guide for the opened-out foldline to keep the binding a constant width.

With the sewing machine, or by hand, and using a matching colour thread, sew the binding to the underside of the mask along the opened-out foldline, sewing the ribbon ties into place and removing the pins as you go.

Fold the binding over the edge of the mask to the front, and pin into place again. Hand-sew the binding in place along the fold. Or topstitch with the sewing machine, aligning the stitching with the edge of the binding on the reverse side to make it less visible. Press the finished piece for a neat edge.

DRAW STRING TOTE BAG

Tote bags are a brilliant thing to have several of. Keep one by your front door, in the car, and in your handbag, so you are always prepared with an eco-friendly, non-plastic bag. This one is super-easy and quick to put together, and you can use a range of natural dye and print techniques, types of fabrics, shapes and sizes to make the most of your collection.

YOU WILL NEED
45 x 55cm (18 x 22in) of dyed fabric
Iron and ironing board
Tape measure or ruler
Dressmaker's pins
Sewing machine
Sewing thread
Large safety pin
Cord or ribbon

DYE MATERIAL Fustic dye powder with iron water added as mordant. See p125 for making a printing ink

DYE METHOD Woodblock printing (see p127–128)

FABRIC Lightweight linen (plant fibre)

MORDANT For linen, use two-step mineral mordant, oak gall, alum and soda ash (see p38)

With this design you don't have to use fabric to the exact dimensions given – just allow 4cm (1½in) on the width and 5cm (2in) on the length for the seam allowances and make the bag whatever size you like.

Lay the fabric out flat on the work surface or an ironing board and press any creases out with the iron.

Make a double hem by folding the sides and bottom of the bag under by 1cm (⅜in) to the wrong side and then fold under again by 1cm (⅜in). This will stop the fabric from fraying. Press the folds with the iron and then pin into place, placing the pins at a right angle to the edge so that the needle can sew over them.

Next create the drawstring channel at the top of the bag by folding the fabric under by 1cm (⅜in) to the wrong side and then under again by 3cm (1¼in) – or make the channel large enough to accommodate your cord. Press the folds with the iron and pin as before. Using the sewing machine, sew the channel in place close to the first fold.

Fold the fabric in half with right sides together, so that the two hemmed sides are aligned, one on top of the other, and are visible on the outside. Move the pins so they are now through all layers, holding the sides together.

Sew each side and bottom seam with a zigzag stitch through the hems, working from the bottom fold and stopping at the bottom of the top hem. Be careful not to sew through the channel at the top, as you need the ends open for the drawstring!

Remove the pins and turn the bag right side out. Use something pointy and blunt to push out the corners into neat points.

Fold over the end of the cord or ribbon and attach the safety pin. Use the safety pin to feed the cord/ribbon through the top channel, right around the top of the bag and out the other end of the channel. Tie the two ends of the drawstring into a knot.

SUPPLIERS

NATURAL DYES
UK
Wild Colours – wildcolours.co.uk
Busy Bees Farm – busybeesfarm.co.uk

USA
Botanical Colors – botanicalcolors.com
Aurora Silk – aurorasilk.com

ECO-CLOTH SUPPLIERS
UK
Cloth House – clothhouse.com
Offset Warehouse – offsetwarehouse.com
Green Fibres – greenfibres.com
Botanical Inks (organic British grown silk) – botanicalinks.com
Bristol Cloth – bristolcloth.co.uk

USA
Aurora Silk – aurorasilk.com
Vreseis (organic colour grown cotton) – vreseis.com

AUS
Beautiful Silks – beautifulsilks.com

ECO-YARNS
UK
Blacker Yarns – blackeryarns.co.uk
Tamarisk – tamariskfarm.co.uk
Cornish Organic Wool – cornishorganicwool.co.uk
Yarn Yarn – yarnyarn.co.uk

USA
The Woolery – woolery.com
Voices of Industry – voicesofindustry.com
Vreseis (organic colour grown cotton) – vreseis.com
Lani's Lana – lanislana.com

ECO-PAPER SUPPLIERS
UK
Eco Craft (recycled) – eco-craft.co.uk
Shepherds (recycled and handmade) – store.bookbinding.co.uk

USA
Eco Paper – ecopaper.com

TRADITIONAL ARTIST SUPPLIES
UK
L Cornelissen & Son – cornelissen.com

OTHER USEFUL AND EDUCATIONAL SITES

Plants For A Future – pfaf.org
Fibershed – fibershed.com
Centre for Sustainable Fashion – sustainable-fashion.com
Cleaner Cotton – sustainablecotton.org
Textile Arts Center – textileartscenter.com
India Flint – indiaflint.com
Slow Fiber Studios – slowfiberstudios.com

INDEX

I have so much gratitude for so many people who have been a part of my journey with natural dyes and this book.

Zena Alkayat, I am so grateful to you for providing me with the opportunity to write this book, and for bringing clarity to my words with your eloquence and clear vision. Your expertise in editing is so gracefully matched with your warmth and humour. Thank you for your commitment to this project and your faith in my work. And for bringing together the dream team for this co-creation.

Kim Lightbody, thank you for your beautiful photography, which has brought this book to life. Thank you Alexander Breeze for your sweet presence and charming style. Claire Rochford for shaping the visuals and flow so well. And to the whole editorial team at Quadrille who have poured over this text and polished the images to perfection.

I'm forever grateful to my family and friends who have nurtured and nourished me with love, care and guidance at every step.

Thank you Mum and Tonia for always being there and Dad for helping to make things happen! Mum – you were my original inspiration for living a sustainable life.

My dear Cassykins, for all of the years of friendship, and the hundreds of onion skins!

Emma Hague, your incredible work in sustainable textiles shines such hope and possibility on what we can do when we have a strong vision and work together to create it. You are a great connector of people, a visionary and a beautifully balanced force of intelligence and compassion. Working with you is such a blessing. Thank you for being an ongoing inspiration and ally.

Louise, you were the original illuminator of this path for me. I'm so grateful for this inspired and right-on introduction and for always showing up when I need you most.

Darling Petronella, thank you for being there and for such nurturing, inspirational, nourishing friendship, excellent ideas and general moving and shaking.

Ped, thank you for all years of friendship and for always hosting me at the Palace!

Sophie HP, for all the gracious hosting throughout the months of crafting this book and for all of your support.

Sofia and Bridie, your gentle patience, support, spirit and sharing of space through this creative process have been so very appreciated.

Tom Beale, for all of the ways you have offered loving kindness and such generous support, I will always be grateful.

Tamara, for sharing your stories and your light.

For all of my teachers, mentors and colleagues who have shared so generously their wisdom, passion, insight and experience with me, in cultivating my understanding of natural materials.

Thank you to Rashid for guiding me into the ancient world of natural dyeing and printing, in what once was the Indus Valley. To Michael for sharing your home, purple potatoes and enchanting natural dyeing wisdom. David Cranswick for being such an inspiring and generous teacher. India Flint for being so true to your values. Cara Marie Piazza, for your fabulous witchcraft. Kathy Hattori, for your kind and generous support and just being such a beautiful soul. Jenny Dean, for lighting the way. Michel Garcia, for simplifying the organic indigo vat dyeing process and making it so accessible.

To my incredible community in Bristol, London and the wider field of sustainable textiles, design, craft, growing and farming. It's an honour and a delight to feel a sense of belonging among you all. And to be surrounded by such incredible visionaries, dreamers, innovators, doers and open-hearted folk.

Lizzie Harrison, for offering your wisdom and support. Dash + Miller, for your generous guidance and knowledge. Fernhill Farm, for being an inspiring wool partner. Old Market Manor, for providing the space for Botanical Inks to grow from. Charlotte and Ela, for your patience! Langfordians, thank you for so much ongoing support and providing space for making a mess. The Ethicurean, thank you for your kind support and encouragement. Mark at Barley Wood Walled Garden, thank you for the rhubarb leaves! Silki at The Forge for creating and sharing such a beautiful space. Feed Bristol, thank you for sharing your space. Flowers From The Plot, thank you for the beautiful flowers. The Cloth House, for the beautiful cloth and just generally existing. Wild Colours, for providing responsibly sourced dyestuffs. Matter Wholefoods, thanks for the onion skins! Chi Wholefoods, for the organic supplies. The Vintage Kitchen Store, Cornelissen & Son and Shepherds Bookbinders for all the beautiful things!

And for all my friends who I have not mentioned who have been there through this creative journey. I thank each and every one of my wonderful students who have attended my workshops, and their willingness to play and experiment with natural dyes. I learn so much from you and through sharing these beautiful techniques with you.

This book is offered in deep love of Earth and belief in the interconnectedness of all things. In dedication to bringing awareness to the way in which we make things, from soil to soil. May we find our way back to living harmoniously on Earth.

Publishing Director Sarah Lavelle
Commissioning Editor Zena Alkayat
Designer Claire Rochford
Photographer Kim Lightbody
Props Stylist Alexander Breeze
Production Director Vincent Smith
Production Controller Tom Moore

Published in 2018 by Quadrille, an imprint of Hardie Grant Publishing

Quadrille
52–54 Southwark Street
London SE1 1UN
quadrille.com

text © Babs Behan 2018
photography © Kim Lightbody 2018
design © Quadrille 2018

ISBN 978 1 78713 156 9

Printed in China